# EXIT!

## 12 Steps to Sell Your Business For the Price You Deserve

JULIE GORDON WHITE

BlueKey Media Group

In Partnership with

Business Coach Press
CALIFORNIA

First Edition Hard Cover

ISBN: 0978962761
ISBN-13: 9780978962760

White, Julie Gordon
Exit! 12 Steps to Sell Your Business for the Price You Deserve - 1st ed.

Published in the United States of America

For information or additional copies address:

Business Coach Press c/o BlueKey Media Group
2390 Domingo Avenue Ste. 230
Berkeley, CA 94705
exitbook@exitjourney.com

# Accolades for the Author

"Working with Julie White to sell my market research company was far easier than I ever imagined. In fact, I was afraid I would be in for a long sales period and a barrage of tasks and inquiries. Julie is so incredibly organized that I was able to bring the paperwork she needed together rather quickly based on her document process. In addition, I was very pleasantly surprised that within a few weeks she brought me multiple offers. The sale of my company happened quickly and efficiently. Throughout the process, Julie was supportive, knowledgeable, and dedicated to securing a good outcome for both me and the buyer."

—S. Fox, Business Seller

"My broker's calm demeanor helped me successfully navigate the complicated process of due diligence culminating with the purchase of a profitable business. Her knowledgeable and calm, no pressure approach was invaluable to helping me reach the decision to purchase my business, and they were responsive from the first email that I sent through the transition of ownership."

—G. Belk, Business Buyer

"Julie has provided excellent service by listening closely to our needs as institutional investors and proposing investment opportunities that fit our criteria. Furthermore, she is a pleasure to work with."

—Jesse Brandl, *Associate, Pacific Community Ventures*

"Thank you so much for going the extra mile with the sale of our company, especially when handling the Phase II environmental matter associated with the building sale. In fact, I have already referred you to our attorney and a business owner colleague."

—A. Cayting, Business Seller

"Exceptional work ethics and follow through. Julie is professional and demonstrates results-driven mentorship to guide business acquisition initiatives."

—Robert Grauer PhD, Business Buyer

"Julie helped several of my clients put their company up for sale. They knew very little about the process so had to be walked through the entire process. She and the people who worked for her were very professional in all areas of the transaction. I can highly recommend her and her team."

—Steven Hilferty, CEO, 8 Secrets Group

"Having worked the escrows for BlueKey for the last 6 years, I find that they are very knowledgeable and experienced in multiple transactions, including assets sales, stock transfers, holding escrows and real estate. As a dual acting Broker they listen carefully to the needs of the parties, and their transactions are always smooth. Julie is a delight to work with, and highly recommended for any business transactions."

—I. Lillenes, Escrow Officer

"Julie is a trusted professional and a delight to work with. I've received nothing but positive feedback from clients

that have worked with her. Julie is my recommended source for business brokerage and pre-sale consulting."
—Chip Doyle, Owner, Sandler Sales Institute

"When I first had the privilege of working with BlueKey, I was not sure what to expect. As time went on, I couldn't believe how lucky I was to work with such a positive and professional broker. She really knows her business and brings so much knowledge and expertise to each transaction. She is a tribute to her profession and I look forward to any opportunity that allows me to be a part of her team."
—R. King, Vice President, Comerica Bank

"Julie has a great method for helping business owners make better decisions about their companies, based on the companies' current value or potential value. Once owners are clear how much their businesses are worth—or could be worth with some actions taken—my work as a business coach becomes easier. Julie's breadth and depth of industry knowledge is impressive, so I can trust her on every evaluation or recommendation."
—Tom Leal, Co-Owner, 8 Secrets Group

"Julie Gordon White has a magnetic personality and a determination to excel in her business practice. Her organization, time management, and thoughtful consideration make her an asset during exquisitely involved business transactions. I do not hesitate to recommend her services to anyone buying or selling a business."
—Sher King, Negotiator & Mediator, Bonde, Inc.

# Dedication and Thanks

I gratefully dedicate this book first and foremost to my loving husband, David, and children Scott, Georgia, and Blake, for putting up with "caving" both in my mind and in my office for painfully long stretches of time in order for me to share my knowledge and heart with the world.

Next, I would never have continued to strive for my own personal pinnacle without my life-long mentor, business partner, and dear friend, Kevin Steele.

Also, huge thanks to the masterminds of my ExecNet and Women Presidents' groups (especially Steve Hilferty, Stu Bolinger, Nina Cooper, Sharon Rubens, Ann Blackburn, Elizabeth Becker and Elizabeth Whitehouse) and also my trusted advisors Ron Clausen, Michelle Heston, Preston Cranford and of course Jim Horan, who never falter on holding my feet to the fire.

To my BlueKey Managing Director Mike Nova for holding down the fort while I was making this happen.

Special thanks to my One Minute Millionaire Mentor Robert G. Allen who graciously invited me into his home and convinced me that my personal light is truly bright enough.

To my brother Ron, who with his support in the pouring rain showed me that I have what it takes to go the distance—26.2 on the marathon course and on the road of life as well.

And last but never least, to my dear parents, Joyce and Ron Gordon. Your unconditional love is the center of my entire being and the reason I am who I am today.

# Table of Contents

## THE ART OF THE DEAL

## WRAPPING IT ALL UP

## CONNECT WITH THE AUTHOR

# Introduction

Most people can't or won't think about how or when they will exit from their business unless they are force to. They know this will be one of the most significant events in their life that will impact them, their family, partners, employees and possibly their community. The continuous postponement of planning the exit from one's business is a serious mistake.

Failing to proactively plan your exit means you run the risk you will be forced to sell your company because of unexpected health, personal or family events, poor economic conditions, poor management decisions, fraud, bankruptcy and other disastrous business ending events. Selling a business under duress is never a happy event. It also may mean the people the most important to you will have to tackle and manage this process because you can't.

Here is the good news! In this book, Julie Gordon White does an amazing job of demystifying and simplifying the process of how to exit from your business. She clearly explains the 12 steps you must take to sell your business for the price you want and deserve. This is a comprehensive "how to" manual that covers the entire process, step by step.

The author immediately answers the questions most sellers what to know like, when is the best time to sell my business? How do I calculate what my business is worth? What is the profile of the buyer who will be willing to buy my business at the price and terms I want and deserve? Plus much more and her explanations are clear and understandable.

Like your business? Not in a hurry to sell?

This is the perfect time to begin to learning the steps and processes on how to exit your business. I encourage you do a quick read of the entire book and then calculate the value of your business using Julie's easy formula. If you are not happy with the result, use this book as a tool to assess your business. Rethink how you are operating your business. Ask yourself what changes can I make that will improve my valuation... then make a plan and begin to implement those changes. I also encourage you to explore the many checklists she provides and begin to make a list of the next steps you are going to take. Be proactive... your business is an important asset!

People who have sold one or more businesses say when they start a new business they immediately begin to think about who the potential buyer(s) is going to be... and then build the business they will want to buy. It is solid advice.

Read EXIT! today. It's a small investment of your time. I promise it will generate an exponential return on your investment. I also think you will enjoy the process.

**Jim Horan, Author, Consultant, Speaker**
**President, The One Page Business Plan Company**

# How to Get the Most Out of This Book *FAST*

After working with literally hundreds of business sellers and buyers over the years, I know you are extremely busy with day-to-day operations, so congratulations for making the decision to read this important book.

By doing so, you are now on the path to understanding how to sell your company—a journey that many business owners don't begin to think about until it's too late and their business is *no longer sellable.*

In order to shorten the learning curve, I compiled all of the critical information presented in the last section titled "Wrapping It All Up." In essence, you don't have to read the entire book if you frequently reference this "toolbox" of information to avoid the costly mistakes that business owners inadvertently make.

The Wrapping It All Up section includes the following:

- All Twenty-Seven Broker's Secrets Noted in the Book
- The Complete Selling Your Business Checklist
- Four Sample Business Valuation Worksheets
- How to Download Your Own FREE Valuation Worksheet
- Eleven Deal-Breakers to Dodge
- My Favorite Business Book Must-Reads
- How to Select a Qualified Business Broker

Having said that, if you really want to ensure that you sell your business for the price you deserve, gift yourself with an afternoon of reading about how to successfully fund the next phase of your life where the daily pressure of running a business no longer weighs heavy on your mind.

In the first three steps of *EXIT!* I will share with you why businesses change ownership (or not), how to determine the best time to sell, and how to value your own company in thirty minutes or less.

From there you'll learn how to get ready for market and how to prepare your financial statements. Then we'll even contemplate the cost benefit of selling your business on your own and—if not—how to assemble your success team.

Once you have a clear overview of the process, we will go deeper and discuss the difference between an asset sale and a stock sale, how to market for buyers, how to manage the offer and due diligence process, and, lastly, how to exit problem-free and with a bank account full of cash.

As I mentioned before, your reward for completing the twelve steps is the toolbox of checklists, all of my broker's secrets, sample valuations sheets, plus a few extra resources to further support your journey.

Finally, after you finish the book, be sure to visit www.exitjourney.com for more tips, tools, videos, and events to help you fast-track your way to *selling your business for the price you deserve.*

Enjoy!

Julie Gordon White

# UNDERSTANDING YOUR OPTIONS

"True generosity must benefit both parties. No woman can control her destiny if she doesn't give *to* herself as much as she gives *of* herself."

~ Suze Orman

# Step One

## Understand Why Businesses Don't Sell and Do Sell

The life of a business owner is both rewarding and *exhausting!* All business owners know that to run a successful company you need to be a great marketer, control your costs, and deliver unbelievable customer service. However, when the time comes to exit your business, lack of preplanning will leave even the best operators hostage to poor financials and bottom-feeding buyers.

As a business owner, you deserve to achieve the highest market price for your company. Begin planning your exit strategy with the same amount of thought and detail that you plan your customer service strategy or craft your marketing plan. By doing so, you will be able to walk away from your company knowing that you created something bigger than yourself and have the financial stability to provide for the next stage of your life.

*Creating and implementing an exit strategy for your business can be the difference between taking a long vacation or retiring with financial freedom after the closing!*

But what if you don't plan? What might your fate be? Instead of a smooth and painless transition out of your company, you may be forced to exit your business by one of the following unfortunate scenarios:

1.  Closing the business due to steadily declining revenues.

2.  Limiting your buyer pool from the open market to a single predatory competitor or undercapitalized employee.

3.  Losing over 60 percent of the sale proceeds due to inadequate tax planning.

4.  Shutting down your business due to a serious accident, grave illness, divorce, or an untimely death of a key employee or partner.

These are the most common exit scenarios for small businesses without an exit plan. Let's explore each of them a bit deeper.

## Closing the Business

This is obviously the most painful option. To be forced to close a business that you have put your heart and soul into developing is a sad misfortune and could have likely been avoided with proper planning.

To receive any cash at all, the owner will probably need to have a fire sale for any remaining assets. You've seen the Must Liquidate signs on retail stores in your neighborhood. You might have also seen ads in online classifieds offering unbelievably cheap or even free furniture and other equipment because business owners have no choice other than to close their doors forever (and may even be forced to file for bankruptcy).

A business owner of a $2 million company once told me, "Having to close my business felt like having a death in my family."

## Unsolicited Offer from a Competitor

I get called in frequently to assist business owners after they have been approached by a competitor seeking to buy them out. In this scenario, the buyer usually has the upper hand. The owner rarely understands what the market value is for the company, let alone how and what to communicate (or hold back) from a buyer that is probably a close competitor.

## BROKER'S SECRET *Competitor Calling*

When a competitor calls, proceed with extreme caution due to confidentiality and never share ANY information with a competitor without expert advice from a business broker, transaction attorney, and/or an accountant.

## Succession Without Adequate Tax Planning

So your daughter decides that she is having a midlife crisis and wants to buy your business. You are thrilled that she wants to continue your dream and so you ask your attorney to draw up a contract. Just before you present her with the agreement, she tells you that she was hoping that you would just *give* her your company (she is your daughter after all!). In both situations STOP! I will probably say this a hundred times in this book (okay, probably not a hundred, but I should):

## It's NOT how much you get, it's how much you KEEP!

If you are not aware of the tax consequences of a parent "gifting" a business to a child, you need to find out ASAP.

Contact your accountant right away before changing the name on the sign out front!

Selling to a child without adequate tax planning isn't the only way to end up giving your business proceeds to Uncle Sam.

If you are a C corporation and you sell only the assets of your corporation and not the stock, you may be subject to paying taxes on the consideration (consideration is cash, loan payments, etc.) received for the sale at the corporate level and then again at the personal level when you take the cash. There are ways to mitigate your tax burden, so spend the time and money to review and understand your options as they relate to the tax consequences of the sale.

## Accident, Illness, Divorce, or Death

Hopefully you have been fortunate enough to identify and develop a key manager for your business. Over time, you have trusted this person with confidential information, given her or him significant responsibility, and, overall, have come to depend on her or him as your right-hand person. If this is your situation, then congratulations. Finding and developing this person is one of the most important activities a CEO can do to allow the company to grow. However, be aware that dependence on a key employee without documented systems in place is very risky. If a competitor steals this person away from you or they strike out on their own, be sure to have your policies, procedures, and systems documented and ready for a new hire to seamlessly step into the role. If you neglect this important process, you may find yourself in a desperate situation, one in which your key manager and chief moneymaker have just walked out the door.

Equally devastating, a sudden illness, divorce, or death of a key employee or partner will have the same effect or greater, so plan for the best but prepare for the worst. Treat your business as if you were planning to franchise it (for information about franchising your business, visit www. franchise.org) and document every single step just like McDonald's does for its franchisees. There's a reason why every burger tastes the same no matter where you go, so take heed and write everything down—today!

Fortunately, for proactive business owners, there are many profitable exit scenarios:

1. Merging with another company

2. Receiving an investment from a private equity group

3. Structuring an Employee Stock Option Plan (ESOP)

4. Supporting a management buyout

5. Tax-advantageous transition of the business to family member(s)

6. Selling the company to a third-party buyer

These exit options are a million times better figuratively and literally.

Now that you understand what you *don't* want to happen and also what you *hope* to happen, you can now see why planning your exit is so important. Simply put, exit planning or lack of, can either make you, save you, or lose you thousands (if not millions) of dollars.

While all of the options above are worthy of their own lengthy discussion, for the purposes of this book, we will focus strictly on number six, the sale of your company to a third-party buyer. After working with hundreds of sellers and buyers, my opinion is that a third-party sale offers you the best chance to receive the maximum price you deserve.

## BROKER'S SECRET *Legacy vs. Cash*

Selling to a third party almost always results in a higher price and better terms, but if you decide to sell to your family, I both respect and applaud you. Remember to do your tax planning and take a lot of pictures the day you hand over the keys.

Before jumping into the details of a planned third-party sale, let's explore the benefits of doing so.

### The Benefits of a Planned Sale of Your Business

A planned sale allows you the opportunity to seek multiple potential buyers in the open market who will often pay a higher price than competitors or employees who don't feel they should pay for infrastructure they already have or helped build.

A planned sale also allows for an owner's financial goals, objectives, and timetable to be achieved and *not* at the mercy of the buyer's financial goals, objectives, and timetable.

Lastly, with a planned sale, you have time to understand the strengths, weaknesses, and opportunities and threats of your company and make changes accordingly with the goal of significantly increasing the final selling price.

Now that you understand the benefits of a planned sale, one of the first critical steps towards achieving your goal is to contemplate and commit to why you have decided to sell at this time.

## Possible Reasons for Selling the Business

With the planned sale of your business, your reason for selling will be one of the most important "trust factors" created to reach agreement with a potential buyer.

Selling your business to an outside buyer begins with a courtship. Don't ask to get married on the first date, and never, ever lie about why you want to get to know them better!

The following exit options are the most common reasons for selling a business to a third party, listed in order of highest credibility:

## Retirement

This is THE very best reason for selling. If you are of retirement age, a buyer will more readily accept that you are selling so you can start enjoying the next phase of your life—not just hiding from problems in the business such as the loss of a customer or key employee.

## Health Issues

Health issues are another legitimate reason to sell. You don't have to divulge all of the details of your personal health situation, but the more forthcoming you are, the greater likelihood that the buyer will believe your reason for your selling along with other critical aspects of the sale.

## Death

Death of an owner or partner is a very unfortunate but legitimate reason for a sale.

## Divorce/Partnership Disputes

Divorce and/or partnership disputes are also legitimate reasons for a sale as long as they significantly affect your ability to operate the business. If you cite this as your reason for sale, make sure you have a good story to tell (and don't mind telling it).

## Loss of Market Share

Be honest about declining sales, because in a challenging economy, you can. Be forthcoming with information, share the down and dirty details, and be prepared to present the plan to help the new buyer grow again as the economy rebounds. Also, be prepared to participate in the financing (promissory note or an earnout—more on these financial instruments later) to reap the upside benefits.

## Burn-Out or "Other Business Interests"

Every business owner gets burned out. After 10+ years of growing, nurturing, and painstakingly building your company you may be at the end of your rope resulting in what I call the "entrepreneur's flu" or burn-out. A sale due to burn-out is often euphemistically marketed by business brokers as "other business interests": however, if you use burn-out to disguise a problem in the business, a buyer will quickly (or eventually—which is even worse) figure it out and your deal will die a slow and painful death.

## Second Generation Not Interested

In our research, we found that only 30 percent of all family-held businesses transfer to the second generation and only 15 percent make it to the third. When the time is right, have a frank conversation with your potential heirs or successors because it's never too early to find out that taking over the family business is *your* dream and not theirs.

## Business Growing Too Fast

This is a great problem to have! This most often occurs in an emerging market or with a hard-driving sales- and marketing-oriented CEO. The hyper growth creates the need for additional capital to finance infrastructure, head count, or improve cash flow. This situation calls more for an investor or equity partner than a sale, so make sure you are clear about what your needs and objectives are.

## Personal Diversification

For some entrepreneurs, businesses are strictly investments, so those business owners will say that they want to diversify their interests to buy something else. To a buyer, this often doesn't make sense. If you sell this asset to buy another, there went your diversification. In a closely held company (owner as the operator) this can be a poor reason for a sale.

So, to recap, make sure your reason for selling is legitimate and your "selling story" is practiced. Answering the "reason for selling question" honestly and convincingly will set the stage for an open and friction-free negotiation.

# Step Two

## Determine Your Ideal Time to Sell

A successful exit plan begins preferably five years before your targeted exit date.

Specifically, here is my **Price You Deserve Formula**:

- **6 months to complete a SWOT (Strengths, Weaknesses, Opportunities, and Threats) analysis of your business**

- **18 Eighteen months to implement SWOT findings to increase profits**

- **3 Years to file profitable Federal Tax Returns**

The bank will require a buyer to provide three years of Federal Tax Returns for *your* business in addition to three years of *the buyer's* personal tax returns in order to secure financing for the purchase. A five-year head start is ideal because a company with growing profits is a bank's dream-come-true—not to mention this will almost always guarantee you multiple offers for your business.

## BROKER'S SECRET *No Financing, No Deal*

If your business's tax returns don't qualify for traditional bank financing, your business may not be sellable, and the only banker left will be the "Bank of First National Seller" (YOU), which is definitely not going to be your first choice.

The next step towards creating an exit strategy is to get your personal financial picture in order.

### Getting Your Personal Retirement Plan in Order

As a business owner and future seller, be sure that you have adequate protection with life insurance, disability insurance, and even business interruption insurance to protect your company in the event that a disaster occurs.

Next, if you haven't already, enlist the services of a tax or transaction accountant familiar with mergers and acquisitions so you can be advised as to the best strategies to minimize the tax consequences of the sale.

Also, if you don't have a relationship with a wealth manager or financial planner, now is a great time to establish one so they can help you maximize the proceeds after the sale. Most business owners' largest asset after their home is their business. Having such a large illiquid asset can be risky. If you are forced to sell after several months or years of minimal profitability, you will not be able to sell for the maximum price or the cash you had anticipated. In preparation, your financial advisor may recommend building up cash reserves, buying other investments, or acquiring real estate to balance out your portfolio. Regardless of the outcome, without a clear understanding of your personal financial picture, you will not be able to make accurate strategic decisions for the future.

Once you understand your personal position, keep in mind four other indicators of good timing:

## 1. Sell When Your Industry Is Hot

You may have heard the quote *"A rising tide lifts all boats."* Is your industry growing? For example, age-wave businesses will grow through increased demand for products and services, so if your business serves the senior or healthcare market your business will most likely grow with that demand. If your business segment is in an area of high growth and demand, position your company positively for a buyer who is interested in your industry.

## 2. Sell When Interest Rates Are Favorable

Remember my comment about financing? If your business has flat to growing sales, is profitable, and your buyer has closely related experience in your industry, then the buyer will have a very high likelihood of securing bank financing to buy your business. When interest rates are low, the cost of money decreases resulting in lower monthly debt payments and a higher return on investment (ROI) for the buyer.

## 3. Sell When Buyers Are Plentiful

Is there gold in layoffs? Possibly! The golden nuggets for you are millions of corporate managers entering the business-buying market. Corporate middle managers and high-level executives are seeking business ownership as a way to secure their future. If they are going to be loyal to a company, it might as well be their own.

---

### BROKER'S SECRET *CORPORATE PARACHUTERS*

Ex-corporate middle managers look great on paper, present well, and have large 401(k)s to secure financing, but they are used to spending other people's money. When it comes time to reach into their own pockets, they may not be able to pull the trigger. Ask questions to uncover their risk tolerance such as, "Were your parents entrepreneurs?" so you don't waste time with someone who will never go all the way to the finish line.

---

Probably and most importantly,

## 4. Sell When Your Business Is Most Profitable

Profitable businesses that are properly priced sell in ANY market. If your business is profitable and interest rates are low, the time to sell your business is NOW!

# Step Three

## Calculate the Fair Market Value of Your Business

Before putting a business on the market, business owners must ask themselves, "How much cash do I want to receive at the closing?" and even go so far as to ask, "What is my pie-in-the-sky premium price?"

Market price is defined by business brokers as the following:

> **"The hypothetical price at which a transaction occurs between a willing buyer and a willing seller, both reasonably informed, neither acting under any compulsion and both of whom have the financial capacity to engage in the transaction."**
> *Source: California Association of Business Brokers*

The translation of that definition of market price is whatever an informed buyer is willing to offer and an informed seller is willing to accept.

That's it.

Keep in mind that you as the seller will have to pay taxes on the proceeds of the sale either as regular income, capital gains, or both. In addition, there will be closing costs, legal fees, accounting fees, and brokerage fees if those industry experts have been engaged.

So remember...

## It's NOT how much you get, it's how much you KEEP!

Let's begin the journey of determining what the potential market value of your company is. You may be thrilled with the result, or you may be unhappy about the truth. This simplified process will serve as an excellent "Back of the Envelope Valuation" for your own peace of mind, but when you are ready to actually sell, make sure you have your business valued by a qualified business broker or Certified Business Appraiser.

---

## BROKER'S SECRET *The 1x Myth*

Contrary to popular belief, a business is rarely valued at 1 times revenue! Don't have your business valued by your accountant (unless they are accredited in business valuation) or your attorney. They may not have access to market comparables (comps) or an understanding of how the business-for-sale market is currently trading.

---

## Valuing Your Business

The foundation of your valuation begins by establishing your "Adjusted Net Profit" or "Seller's Discretionary Earnings" (SDE) based on your earnings plus other key factors. Businesses with revenues over $10,000,000 are often valued on a multiple of EBITDA (earnings before interest, taxes, depreciation, and amortization); however, for our purposes, we will focus on SDE.

## Let's look at each of the key elements of a Back of the Envelope Valuation.

1. Seller's Discretionary Earnings (SDE)
2. Value of Tangible Assets
3. Value of Intangible Assets
4. Management Team in Place
5. Customer Concentration
6. Comparable Sales
7. Replacement Value of Equipment Adjustment
8. Full-Time Owner Adjustment
9. Market Lease Adjustment
10. Market Segment
11. Territory/Franchise/Distribution Rights
12. Documents Systems

### Seller's Discretionary Earnings (SDE)

SDE is the heart of the valuation. Unless the business value is based on proprietary intellectual property—a technology company, for example—all small businesses will sell for a multiple of Seller's Discretionary Earnings or SDE. SDE is calculated by adding owner's salary, owner's payroll taxes, health benefits, retirement benefits, financial perks, depreciation, amortization, and non-reoccurring expenses (a one-time expense) to the net income stated on the profit and loss statement or preferably the tax returns (because a bank will base its valuation of your business on tax returns). By adding these items back to the financial statement (called "add-backs" or "adjustments"), a buyer will have a better idea of how much income he or she can expect to receive when he or she takes over the company.

## Value of Tangible Assets – Equipment

This is the value of the depreciated equipment included in the sale. The depreciated value will be found on your most current balance sheet under the assets section or on your tax returns on the depreciation schedule. A buyer will not pay "replacement cost" or today's retail cost for a piece of equipment that you have used for a period of time. Expect to only receive liquidation value for most items.

## Value of Tangible Assets – Inventory

An ongoing debate amongst business brokers is whether or not to include inventory in the price or add it to the multiple of SDE. The argument is that the business could not have generated the revenues without the inventory so a "normalized" or usual working amount should be included at no additional cost to the buyer. Others believe that inventory should be added in addition to the SDE because a buyer doesn't necessarily have to purchase the entire inventory on hand at the time of sale (especially if it is old, damaged, or otherwise unsellable). Either way, I would encourage you to at least include a minimal amount to get the buyer off to a successful start. The buyer probably owes you money after the closing, so it's to your benefit as well.

## Value of Tangible Assets – Receivables

Including receivables in the sale of a business is another frequently negotiated item during a sale. We will discuss an asset versus stock sale later, but generally, receivables are not included in an asset sale but are included in a stock sale. It is common for a buyer to negotiate that the receivables equal to one month's working capital (break-even cash flow for one month) be included. Receivables are the same as cash so they can generally be added to the calculated multiple of SDE to arrive at a final price.

## Value of Intangible Assets

Intangible assets are often lumped together as "goodwill." If we look closer at what intangibles make up goodwill, the list might include reputation, copyrights, patents, food recipes, proprietary systems, customer lists, and other "soft" assets. For the purposes of our Back of the Envelope Valuation, we will consider that the calculated SDE includes all the possible individual elements of goodwill.

## Management Team in Place

Buyers will pay more for a company that is not owner-dependent. An experienced senior manager and/or key employee(s) will lessen the fears that a buyer may have about all of the knowledge and history of the business walking out the door with the seller after the sale.

## Customer Concentration

Analyze your top ten clients to understand clearly how much revenue each contributes to your gross sales. If one customer contributes more than 10 percent of sales, you may have a customer concentration issue. If your top ten customers contribute more than 30 percent of sales, you may have an even larger issue that should be dealt with before putting your company on the market.

---

**BROKER'S SECRET** *CUSTOMER CONCENTRATION*

Customer concentration is a deal killer. Diversify immediately or postpone your sale. You probably won't be able to sell anyway and you definitely won't receive the maximum price for your company.

---

You probably have a long and trusted relationship with your largest customers, but the buyer will not. I promise you, no amount of convincing will make a buyer think that he or she will inherit this relationship with the sale. Start securing long-term written and transferable agreements with large customers and/or begin adding many medium and smaller customers to diversify your revenue base.

## Comparable Sales

Using comparable sales—or comps—is an important way that business brokers and owners can compare their business valuation to the sold price for other businesses in the same industry with similar revenue and SDE. Two great businesses-for-sale websites are www.bizbuysell.com and www.bizquest.com. You can search these sites with keywords for your industry and see sold price and multiples as well as other similar businesses currently on the market. These websites also have other helpful tools and articles for both business sellers and buyers.

---

**BROKER'S SECRET** *ASKING VS. SELLING*

When researching comparables currently being advertised, remember that the asking price is not the final selling price, so don't set false pricing expectations for your business based on someone else's false expectations.

---

## Replacement Value of Equipment Adjustment

If you have outdated equipment that will need to be replaced, keep in mind that this capital expenditure will be deducted from your SDE—usually charged against the SDE for the current year.

## Market Lease Adjustment

Do you own your building? If you do, are you charging your business fair market rent? If you are not, a fair market adjustment will have to be made if you plan to rent the building back to the buyer at a different price than you rent it to yourself—whether up or down. If the space is large, this can be a significant adjustment so plan ahead and charge yourself properly after discussing the tax consequences with your CPA.

## Full-Time Owner Adjustment

It is the expectation of most small business buyers to initially operate the company themselves, unless they plan to merge the business with their existing company to create economies of scale. For the purposes of our Back of the Envelope Valuation, we will plan for one full-time owner. If you are the only owner of your company, no adjustment is necessary. If your business is owned by more than one working owner, you will need to replace all but one working owner with employees. Two half-time owners can be replaced with one full-time employee, etc.

## BROKER'S SECRET *Family on the Payroll*

Non-working family members on the payroll is cash to the bottom line and they don't need to be replaced/adjusted for. Just be sure that you can prove to your potential buyer that they truly don't work in the business or add value to the business whatsoever.

## Market Segment

If your business is in an easy-to-understand industry, it will automatically widen your buyer pool. If your business operates in an extremely complex niche in which very few buyers will have related experience, the result may be a limited pool of buyers. Neither factor means that you need to change your business model, but you should be aware of your market position and begin thinking of ways to add value and identify who your best potential buyer might be.

## Territory Rights and Exclusive Agreements

If your business is a franchise or distributor, it will be important to consider the length remaining on your exclusive agreement. Additional factors include territory exclusivity, lack of exclusivity, preferred vendor arrangements, and advantageous pricing to name a few of the possible elements of such agreements.

## Documented Systems

I can hear you groaning! We already touched on this, but to refresh your memory...

All business owners have this pesky, time-consuming, but yet oh-so-important item on their to-do list (and if you don't you better add it ASAP). Documented systems are definitely an intangible asset, but if you want to push your valuation to the premium range, find a way to document each step that you and your team take.

Start by giving each employee a simple pad of paper and have each person spend a few minutes each day writing down what they did during the course of the day. No priority list or fancy matrix required (that's your task—after all, the employees did all the heavy lifting making the list!). This will give you a huge head start towards compiling the data in an electronic format that can be shared with a buyer should the buyer purchase your company. Documented systems give a buyer a sense of confidence that the business has been operated in an orderly and systematic way. This confidence boost will go a long way toward substantiating the buyer's inclination to pay you the maximum price, which is always your ultimate goal.

Okay, the moment you have been waiting for...

## The Back-of-the-Envelope Valuation Formula

**Profit + Owner Benefits + Depreciation + Amortization + Interest = (SDE) x 2x to 4x Multiple = Fair Market Price Range**

### BROKER'S SECRET BOEV *Formula*

A formula this important bears repeating....

Profit + Owner Benefits + Depreciation + Amortization + Interest = (SDE) x 2x to 4x Multiple = Fair Market Price Range

Now I can almost hear you saying, "This is great, but how do I know if I should multiply the SDE by two, three or four?"

Most small businesses sell on a multiple of 2.5 to 3 times SDE. In fact, there was a study that showed that the average sold multiple for small businesses is 2.3 and hasn't changed since the 1960s.

While this is a true statistic, if your business has an easily verifiable SDE of $100,000 or more (no marginal owner perks added to the net profit such as visits to big box retailers, salaries for nannies, trips that weren't even in the convention city—I have seen it all), you can be very confident of a 3x multiple, and possibly push it to 4 (or maybe even 5 for certain industries) if your SDE is $500,000 or greater.

**For your reference, in the Wrapping It All Up section in the back of the book you will find SDE calculation worksheets for four sample businesses with revenues ranging from $500,000 to nearly $5,000,000.**

## Actual Vs. Pie-in-the-Sky

After determining your Back of the Envelope Valuation, compare the current value of your business to your target exit date and premium price expectations. Is your premium price realistic? Is the time frame realistic to reach the necessary sales levels and profitability to achieve that price? In order for you to reach your goals, all of these elements must come together.

If the pieces of the puzzle don't fit, review your SWOT analysis again, comparing it with the list of valuation factors above. From there, put a plan in place to improve the profitability and goodwill of your company ASAP to achieve your ultimate selling goal—maximum market price—which is the price you deserve!

# GOING
# TO
# MARKET

"Do the right thing and the money will come."
~ Gun Denhart, founder,
Hanna Anderson Corp.

# Step Four
## Get Market Ready

After you have determined the approximate market value of your company and are comfortable with the potential proceeds of the sale, it's time to go to market.

As you remember from Step One, the first significant step towards going to market is to have a credible reason to sell because without it, a buyer will be distrustful of all information you provide thereafter.

What is your "Reason for Selling Story"? Take a few minutes now and write down your one-minute elevator pitch as to why you have decided to put your business on the market. To help you, below is a checklist with additional space for your personal story.

### Selling Story Checklist

I am selling my business now because of the following reasons:

### Strong Reasons to Sell

☐ Retirement
☐ Health Issues
☐ Partnership Dispute
☐ Divorce
☐ Death
☐ Business Growing Too Fast

## Weak Reasons to Sell

- ☐ Loss of Market Share
- ☐ Burn-out
- ☐ Second Generation Not Interested
- ☐ Personal Diversification
- ☐ Business Growing Too Fast

Your Story

_____

_____

_____

_____

_____

_____

_____

Once your story is set and you can share it confidently, you are ready to move on to your pricing strategy.

## Pricing Strategy

When pricing your business for sale, understand that the more reasonably your business is priced, the faster your business will sell. Buyers will pay for a justifiable multiple of SDE plus tangible assets.

Buyers will NOT pay for the following:

1. How much debt you owe on the business or need to pay off personally or

2. How much you "need" for retirement

These numbers are of no concern to a buyer and have no bearing on the business valuation.

## BROKER'S SECRET *PRICING STRATEGY*

Your debts or your retirement income needs are not a buyer's concern and should not be a significant factor when determining your pricing strategy.

If you have done your pre-work and have received an Opinion of Value or certified appraisal for your business, you know what your business is probably worth. You don't need to share the report with a potential buyer, but if you price the business close to the range suggested, I would definitely consider sharing the valuation. The report will be a powerful tool to help you hold your ground when the buyer wants to negotiate on the price. Needless to say, if you price the business higher, I would keep the valuation to myself!

Psychologically, people like to negotiate everything they buy on the open market, so leave room for a little back and forth between parties. Also remember that you will have closing costs related to the sale (taxes on the proceeds, legal fees, accounting fees, broker, and escrow fees) but know that the price should not exceed a range more than 15 percent of the valuation or you will quickly become unattractive to potentially qualified buyers.

### Pre-Qualify Your Business for Financing

If a deal can't be financed, you probably don't have a deal.

A banker will analyze the financability of your business based on the following:

1. Financial strength of the business's previous three fiscal years

2. Financial strength and credit score of the buyer

3. Related industry experience of the buyer

The banker will use these criteria to analyze the business and the buyer's combined ability to repay the loan. Specifically, a bank will want to ensure that the cash flow from the business will cover the expenses of the business, the debt service (the loan payment to the bank), and the buyer's personal monthly expenses by 125 percent.

For example in simple terms, if the loan payment is $10,000 per month, the business must generate cash flow of a minimum of $12,500 to cover the payment plus any personal expenses of the buyer. The cash flow must equal at least 125 percent so the bank will feel confident that the buyer will not need to withdraw cash from the business to cover personal liabilities.

If the business does not generate adequate income to ensure that the buyer has a living wage and that the new business can meet its monthly expenses including the loan payment, the bank will not finance the sale.

Before I move on, I want to make a quick comment about SBA loans or loans backed by the Small Business Administration (more information at www.sba.gov).

Most bank loans for the purchase of small businesses are facilitated by loans that have been guaranteed to the bank by the Small Business Administration, often referred to as the SBA.

Contrary to popular belief, the SBA does not lend money.

The SBA is a federal government program that guarantees a portion of the loan if the bank lends the money based on the established SBA criteria. The SBA usually guarantees 80 percent of the purchase price (the balance is paid by the buyer or a combination of the buyer's down payment and a seller's promissory note), which gives the lending bank the confidence to make the loan because its exposure to risk if the buyer defaults is very limited.

You should only pre-qualify your business with a "Preferred" SBA Lender such as Wells Fargo (www.wellsfargo.com), UPS Capital, or local community bank with preferred SBA status. These lenders actively pursue small business loans, and because they have received "preferred status" they have already been vetted by the SBA and are able to make loan decisions at their local level versus a non-preferred bank that must send all packages to Washington for approval. There is a list of all preferred lenders on the SBA website.

---

**BROKER'S SECRET** *GROWTH IS GOOD*

Declining revenue is a deal killer! If you have a large one-time expense such as a large equipment purchase, the bank may allow you to add that income back to your Seller's Discretionary Earnings, but be prepared for an uphill battle. Banks like flat or growing sales so monitor your profit and loss statements on a monthly basis *at minimum.*

---

Another key financing component to achieving your highest price is for the seller to carry a promissory note, also known as seller financing, making you the banker for a certain portion of the purchase price.

## Promissory or Seller's Note

A typical Promissory or Seller's Note will be 10 percent on the low end to 50 percent on the high end of the total purchase price. The size of the note will tend to be more if the business is a service-related company with little to no tangible assets such as equipment and inventory.

The note should be secured by the assets of the business and personally guaranteed by the buyer.

By offering to carry a note, the seller demonstrates to the buyer that she believes in the business and that she will remain financially invested in the success of the company after the sale. Sellers that carry a partial note often achieve a higher final selling price than those who settle for a potentially discounted "all cash" price.

Carrying a note can seem like a risky proposition, and, truthfully, it is. If the buyer is unsuccessful at running the business and defaults in the process, the seller's only recourse is to take back a potentially worthless business and pursue the buyer for the balance of the note (and you will most definitely be in line, referred to as "second position" or "subordinated" to the bank).

However, by financing a portion of the deal, if all goes as well as everyone hopes, you have now just increased the purchase price of your business.

For example, you agree to sell your business for $1,000,000, and the buyer agrees to pay you $700,000 as the down payment with the balance to be paid in the form of a promissory note for $300,000 plus 7 percent interest over sixty months. The final consideration (cash) you will receive upon full payment of the note will be an additional $131,650.21!

| | |
|---|---|
| Sale Price: | $1,000,000 |
| Down Payment: | $700,000 |
| Seller's Note: | $300,000 |
| Interest: | $131,650.21 |
| Total Consideration: | $1,131,650.21 |

If you do decide to carry a note, be sure to qualify the buyer as rigorously as a bank would. Ask to review their credit rating and three years of personal tax returns before signing on the bottom line.

## Facilities Lease

Equally important to profitability in getting your deal done is the building lease. When a business changes hands, an important element for a new buyer is to be able to secure a long-term lease, preferably for five to ten years with one or two five-year options, at market rate or lower.

As a seller, if at all possible, try not to assign your existing lease even if the remaining term would be advantageous for the buyer. By assigning the lease, you, as the leaseholder, will most likely remain financially responsible for the rent whether the new buyer pays or not. Unfortunately, in most situations, assignment is the only option and the landlord will rarely release the seller from their financial obligation. To make things worse, if the buyer isn't able to receive financial approval from the landlord, or if the new rent proposed will significantly decrease the profitability of the business, your deal will come to a screeching halt.

For the buyer, an assignment is often best because the approval process is easier and the buyer has you as a built-in free consultant for the life of the existing lease (you want to make sure they are successful and pay the rent don't you?). Either way, lease negotiation can make or break a transaction and it is best to know the landlord's intentions as soon as you make the decision to sell.

## BROKER'S SECRET *LANDLORDS*

Landlords are deal killers too! Many business owners don't want to advise the landlord that they are selling the business, which is a major mistake. The statement "approval will not unreasonably be withheld" is written into 99 percent of all of the commercial leases. The only thing they don't tell you is that they can be so unreasonable with their terms that the buyer may reject the landlord AND your business! Be brave; notify the landlord of your intentions before you go to market so at least you can deal with any potential roadblocks before they become insurmountable.

## Gathering Your Selling Documents

A smooth launch to any project requires researching and collecting the data that will be necessary to successfully complete the task. The same is true when getting started with the sale of your company.

In order to assist your support team in preparing your selling documents, you should keep copies of the following documents in a central location:

1. Most recent business valuation or appraisal
2. Year-end profit and loss statements and balance sheets for the last three years
3. Federal Corporate Tax Returns for the last three years
4. Facilities lease or appraisal on your business real estate if you own it and plan to sell it with the business
5. Equipment List
6. Inventory List
7. Organizational Chart
8. Customer Concentration Analysis Report
9. Business Plan and Marketing Plan
10. Policy and Procedures Manual

Having these documents in a central location and regularly updated will save you hours of hunting and copying when the time comes to go to market. Start now, update regularly, and you'll feel confident and powerful when you are eventually asked to share.

Okay, you are almost ready to go to market, but before moving on, we need to spend time on a very sensitive, but critical subject—your financial statements.

# Step Five

## Prepare Your Financial Records

Sharing your financial statements can either be a shining moment within the selling process or it can be as uncomfortable as standing naked in the middle of Times Square at lunchtime. I can't stress this enough:

### Clean up your financial statements now—not when you are In the middle of your deal!

Clean financials get purchased, financed, and live happily ever after, so let's talk about the definition of "clean."

### Record All Sales and Expenses

Now is definitely not the time to hide revenue and expenses from the Internal Revenue Service. All income generated by the business should be credited to the business. A buyer will not pay you for revenue that the buyer can't verify, and they will definitely penalize you (it erodes trust) if they determine that you are hiding income and expenses related to the business.

### Eliminate Co-Mingling of Business and Personal Assets

Remove any personal expenses from your financial statements. Do not pay business bills with personal checks.

Do not pay personal expenses from your business account. Keep a very clear line between business transactions and personal transactions.

## Eliminate "Marginal Perks"

Is your business paying for your health club membership, nanny, housekeeper, or other non-business related expenses? If so, don't expect a buyer to give you credit for these expenses as additional profit to the company unless you can produce a receipt for each one, and even if you can, a bank will not accept marginal perks as additional profit. The bottom line: don't do it. Or at least stop three years before you want to sell.

## Compliance with Taxing Authorities

During the selling process, all taxes must be filed and paid on time. Tax returns are considered the final word for the bank and a buyer (who inflates their revenue to pay more taxes?). Make sure your taxes are correct and readily available. If a bank finances your deal, the lender will request that you allow them to pull official tax return transcripts directly from the Internal Revenue Service so be prepared and file on time.

## Scrub the Balance Sheet

The balance sheet is a snapshot on a given day of the health of your business. If your accountant has left old liabilities (debts) or old assets (old equipment, loan to the shareholder, written off receivables, etc.) on the balance sheet for one reason or another, now is the time to remove them. In a stock sale, you will literally negotiate a new balance sheet so you want to be sure the starting point of the negotiation is accurate.

## Do Your Own Due Diligence

Lastly, put yourself in the buyer's shoes. If you were buying your business, would you find your financials honest, verifiable, and easy to understand? If not, keep scrubbing until you can honestly sell your business to yourself! Most businesses use QuickBooks (www.quickbooks.com) for their bookkeeping system. QuickBooks is easy to use (software or online version), easy to produce reports, and easy to share with your accountant. Your buyer, your CPA, your broker, and your bank account will love you for it.

The last step in preparing for a sale is assembling your success team. You rarely get a second chance to sell your only business, so you need to invest in the experts who can advise and facilitate your transaction in a trustful and knowledgeable manner.

But before you assemble your team, you might be considering something else…

# Step Six

## Understand the Pros & Cons of "For Sale By Owner"

Not that I am biased, but this chapter will be very short! Unless you have a very small business (sales of $100,000 or less), I would not suggest that you sell your business yourself.

When selling "your baby" or something that is about as close to you as your real child or beloved pet, how will you be able to maintain the strictest confidence so your employees don't find out and get nervous and quit? Or even worse, what if your customers find out, get nervous, stop buying from you, and then tell your competitors you are selling?!

Also, how removed can you be when negotiating the terms and price for your baby? Most business owners think that their best buyer is a competitor and, truthfully, a competitor may be your only buyer. However, without a qualified business broker researching and confidentially marketing to first-time buyers who will pay a premium for your business, how will you ever know? There's that problem about confidentiality again, too.

Lastly, it's hard enough to operate a business and possibly a family, let alone try to manage a sale while trying to keep the other two running smoothly. In the long run, you are better off focusing on keeping the business growing and profitable during the sale than trying to save the broker's fee.

But just in case you want try it, email me at Julie@exitjour-
ney.com and I'll send you my article "11 Landmines to Avoid
When Selling Your Business" that was printed in *Enterprising
Woman Magazine* (www.ew.com). And be sure to keep my
email address because I know you'll be contacting me for
another reason soon after!

Okay, getting back to the professional sale of your business (I couldn't resist), let's talk about assembling the team
that can make your exit dreams come true.

# Step Seven

## Assemble Your Selling Success Team

### Selling Success Team

Your success team should include a business broker or intermediary, a tax and transaction accountant, a wealth manager, a business banker, and a transaction attorney.

### Business Broker or Intermediary

A business broker or a business intermediary perform the same duties but focus on different deal sizes. Brokers usually specialize in transactions less than $10 million and intermediaries usually facilitate deals between $10 million and $100 million. Transactions over $100 million are handled by investment bankers.

The importance of engaging a broker or intermediary is to ensure that the sale of your business is managed confidentially and your proceeds are maximized. Typical broker fees range between 10 percent and 12 percent of the final selling price (with no upfront fee), with a declining scale as the price increases beyond one million dollars. Keep in mind that a well executed deal including pre-market planning, tax planning, creative buyer marketing, and expert deal management will more than pay for your broker and your success team fees.

A broker or intermediary will act as the project director or quarterback, coordinating all interaction with your accountant, banker, wealth manager, and attorney. If you do not have existing relationships with these key advisors, your broker will introduce you to trusted professionals that they have most likely teamed up with successfully in the past.

The five most important elements that your broker brings to the table are the following:

1. Helping you establish a fair market price range

2. Maintaining the confidentiality of your sale while simultaneously identifying and introducing qualified buyers

3. Allowing the seller to remain focused on running the business and keeping the revenues steady during the selling process

4. Suggesting creative deal management strategies to create a win-win outcome for all

5. Keeping all players focused and moving forward through the complex and emotional process, all the way to the closing table

When choosing a broker, consider the following:

1. Ask for references from previous sellers and buyers

2. Ask which professional organizations the broker belongs to and any certifications earned from those organizations

3. Ask if the broker will "cooperate or co-broker" (work with and share fees) with another broker who may have a buyer

4. Ask if the broker will represent you exclusively or both parties as a dual agent

5. Ask how the broker will market the business for sale

6. Determine how frequently the broker will communicate with you regarding the status of your transaction

If you are happy with the responses you receive and feel that you can work closely and honestly with this person for the next seven to twelve months, you probably have a match.

## Tax Accountant

Remember this statement?

### It's NOT how much you get, it's how much you keep!

This is the reason you need to have a very experienced and knowledgeable tax accountant on your team. Your personal CPA may or may not be this person. An accountant who understands tax management strategies with the sale of a business can save you thousands or even possibly hundreds of thousands of dollars in taxes, so choose this team member carefully.

## Wealth Manager/Financial Planner

Having a trusted wealth manager on your side flows directly from your tax accountant. You need to understand tax management strategies before your business goes on the market. Once your business sells, you should already have a plan in place to ensure that your after-tax proceeds go to work for you immediately.

## Business Lender or Banker

With the assistance of your broker, your business should be pre-qualified for SBA financing so a buyer who will become a borrower will know in advance how much cash is required to purchase your business. If you already bank with a preferred SBA lender, you should start there because they are already familiar with your business and may be more likely to lend.

## Transaction Attorney

All deals should be reviewed by an experienced transaction attorney before being agreed to and signed by a seller. Your current attorney may or may not be a transaction attorney, so make sure your legal representation has experience reviewing Buy/Sell Agreements.

Now that you have done the hard work of preparing your business for sale, you are finally ready to go to market and are positioned to achieve your maximum price.

But before you do, let's go down one more path and touch briefly on the complicated process of determining whether you should seek an asset sale or stock sale if your business is incorporated.

# Step Eight

## Stock Sale vs. Asset Sale and the Tax Considerations

The tax consequences of any sale are very complicated, but for the purposes of this book, I want to give you a general understanding so you can position your business to be as attractive for a buyer as possible.

I will also remind you that before you decide to sell your company, be sure to sit down with your knowledgeable tax advisor to understand the tax consequences of the sale of your company, particularly as it relates to an asset or stock sale (I know I'm starting to sound redundant, but it's *that* important!).

> ### BROKER'S SECRET *STOCK WARNING!*
>
> Business owners, do not try this on your own! Speak to an experienced advisor before attempting to sell stock!

The discussion between seller and buyer about an asset sale versus a stock sale will be based on the following:

1. The tax consequences of the sale for both the buyer and the seller

2. The assumption or not of liabilities by the buyer

3. The ability to transfer key contracts and or licenses from the seller to the buyer

Generally, a buyer wants to purchase assets because there are no liabilities associated with the sale, and often a seller wants to sell stock in order to minimize the tax consequences of a sale.

Depending on the type of business entity and the assets involved, an asset sale or a stock sale can be advantageous to either side; however, it is critical for both buyer, seller, and their advisors to analyze the best structure of a sale that achieves the goals of both parties.

## Sole Proprietor and/or Partnership

If you are a sole proprietor, your company is not incorporated. You receive income from the net profits of the business. At the end of the year, net profits flow to your personal tax return through a Schedule C as ordinary income and you pay taxes on the total amount personally.

In the event of a sale, you will sell the assets of your business (there is no stock because you are not incorporated) and the proceeds will be taxed as a capital gain and/or ordinary income based on the amount between what you received for the assets (the sale price) and the price you paid for them (as booked on your depreciation schedule).

This structure is advantageous for both seller and buyer to execute an asset sale.

## LLC or LLP

Unlike a sole proprietorship, your business is a corporate entity and your shareholders are called members. Like a sole proprietor or partnership, your income and the proceeds of the sale will pass through from the business's tax return to each member personally and will be taxed as a capital gain and/or ordinary income.

This structure is generally advantageous for both seller and buyer to execute an asset sale.

## Subchapter S Corporation (S Corp)

If your company is a Subchapter S Corporation, you elected Subchapter S after you incorporated as a C Corporation.

By making this election, the income from the business passes through to the shareholders directly from the corporate tax return on a Schedule K-1, and the shareholder pays tax personally on the income generated from the company.

This structure is generally advantageous for both seller and buyer to execute an asset sale; however, buyer and seller still may have conflicting interests in opting for a stock or asset transaction. This requires careful planning and negotiation.

## C Corporation

If your business is incorporated and you have not elected Subchapter S (a regular corporation), you are organized as a C Corporation.

With a C Corporation, any and all income to the corporation, including proceeds of an asset sale, is taxed at the corporate level and then taxed a second time once received by the shareholder. This means that the proceeds that you receive for the sale of your company may be taxed twice, reducing the final cash in your pocket at closing up to 60 percent!

This structure is NOT advantageous for both seller and buyer to execute an asset sale.

In order for a seller to reduce the tax liability on a sale, the seller will prefer to sell the stock of the corporation (stock sale) reducing the tax consequences by approximately 30 percent.

A buyer, on the other hand, generally does not want to buy the stock of a corporation because when a buyer buys stock, the buyer is purchasing not only the assets, but also the liabilities of the corporation, both known and unknown.

Liabilities can include unpaid debts, employment agreements and benefits, warranties, unpaid taxes, and any other known or unknown liability.

Additionally, if a buyer purchases stock, they cannot "step up" (or increase the tax basis) the assets they are buying, which reduces the ability for the buyer to benefit from depreciating the assets of the corporation any further.

On the other hand, a buyer may need to purchase stock so as not to disturb any potential key contracts or licenses in place that are owned or assigned to the corporation directly. In this case, the buyer will have to weigh the benefits and risks of buying the stock of the corporation or not. As the seller, be prepared to provide representations and warranties to increase the comfort of your buyer that to the best of your knowledge, there are no outstanding liabilities and if there are, you will compensate the buyer to the extent agreed upon in the purchase agreement.

## BROKER'S SECRET *TAX MITIGATION*

Your experienced transaction accountant and transaction attorney will counsel you on tax-saving deal strategies such as allocating a portion of the proceeds to employment and or consulting agreements, personal goodwill, and other tax management strategies which will more than pay for their fees.

# THE
# ART
# OF
# THE
# DEAL

"It's far better to buy a wonderful company at a fair
price than a fair company at a wonderful price."
~Warren Buffet, Chairman and CEO,
Berkshire Hathaway

# Step Nine
## Marketing for Buyers

In order to successfully market your business, your broker will create marketing materials to be reviewed by qualified buyers.

The marketing materials are commonly referred to as an Investment Summary, Memorandum of Offering, Confidential Business Review, or Marketing Book.

These marketing materials can be as short as a single page for a small business and as long as twenty to fifty pages for a multi-million-dollar business. The book will contain pertinent information that a buyer will want to know in order to make an informed decision about buying your business. Typical sections of a Confidential Business Review include the following:

- Business Overview
- Summary Financial Statements
- Products and Services
- Competition
- Customer Concentration Analysis
- Organizational Chart
- Equipment List
- Photos

Once you have approved the marketing materials your broker has prepared for your business, your broker will begin the search for buyers that are both financially and professionally qualified. A bank may only lend to a buyer that has a background and experience very closely related to your industry, so brokers have their work cut out for them looking for that perfect needle in the haystack.

Your broker's research and marketing efforts might include the following:

- Researching an in-house database for existing buyer relationships that might be a match

- Advertising on business-for-sale websites such as www.bizbuysell.com or www.bizquest.com without disclosing the name of the business or any details that might allow an industry competitor to identify the business—often called a "blind ad"

- Sending a blind profile of the business to other business brokers or intermediaries in the event that they have a client who might be interested in your business

- Sending letters of interest with follow-up calls to industry competitors in distant geographic areas that might benefit by gaining access to the business's market

- Placing online ads in industry trade publications

## BROKER'S SECRET *BROKER COOPERATION*

Business brokers, unlike real estate agents, do not have an official Multiple Listing Service (MLS) and do not automatically "cooperate" or "co-broker," meaning share fees, with other business brokers. The reason stated is usually based on protecting confidentiality, which can be a valid reason, but this is an important strategy to discuss with your broker. You should ask your broker directly, "Do you cooperate with other brokers?" If the answer is no, you should ask why and also know that it is within your right to request that they do.

Once a buyer is identified and is interested in learning more about your business, the broker will ask the potential buyer to sign a confidentiality agreement or non-disclosure agreement (NDA) and also complete a personal financial statement. There is no reason to share your confidential business information with a buyer who will not sign these documents. In fact, it means that that person or entity is not a real buyer! Your best buyer prospects can range from qualified individuals to small investment groups or private equity groups, and they all know that they must sign an NDA.

In a challenging financing market, banks scrutinize a buyer's qualifications even more than usual. So in this situation, a competitor may be the only buyer for your business. However, I caution you about telling your competitors that your business is for sale even if they sign a confidentiality agreement.

Think about it—wouldn't you be really excited to learn the ins and outs of your closest competitors under the guise of potentially buying them? Of course you would never share what you learned, mostly because you know that they would sue for breach of confidentiality, but at a minimum, just knowing a competitor's strengths and weaknesses is a great strategic advantage. So as a seller, think twice—maybe three times—before courting a direct competitor!

By the way, I place employees in the same category as competitors. Rarely can employees of a small business make the shift from employee to owner or they probably would have broken off and started their own business already.

If the company has a true middle-management layer, a management buyout is not only possible, but may be a great tax mitigation strategy for you if done properly. A successful management buyout requires time, trust, and profits, so make sure all three legs of the stool are solid before you share your plans to sell.

Once an interested buyer has been identified and they have signed a confidentiality agreement, submitted their personal financial statement, and have reviewed the marketing materials, the next probable step is an in-person meeting or conference call with you and your broker.

## BROKER'S SECRET *MULTIPLE OFFERS*

Unlike buyers for a house, it is very unlikely that you will have multiple offers for your business unless it is very profitable with very clean books in a growing industry.

Before you meet your buyer, you should understand why buyers buy.

## So Why Do Buyers Buy?

1. To avoid the risks of start-ups or slow organic expansion

2. To grow faster by acquiring new products, technology, or market share

3. To acquire an established presence or strengthen position in a new geographic market

4. To acquire undervalued assets

5. To achieve the American dream of being self-employed

Let's dig into each of these reasons a little deeper.

## Avoid the Risks of Start-Ups or Organic Expansion

Experienced entrepreneurs know how difficult it is to start a business from zero. You probably remember that it takes hours and hours of dedicated thought, implementation, mistakes, and correction. If a buyer has started a business and failed, or started a business and sold it, they understand the value of an established entity. They will value all elements of the infrastructure you have created and will pay you a fair price for your enterprise. They also have the ability to perform, or as brokers like to say "pull the trigger," and make an offer if most of the information they learn about your business fits their criteria.

## Achieve Growth More Rapidly by Acquiring New Products, Technology or Markets

Once a business has achieved the milestone of a million dollars in sales, owners begin looking for ways to grow faster and easier than it took them to get to the first million, so acquisition often becomes a key strategy. By acquiring a new product line, technology, or market share, a similar business with a strong cash position can be an attractive buyer candidate.

## Acquire an Established Presence or Strengthen Market Position

We are now getting into competitor territory, so qualify the buyer thoroughly and advance information slowly. If you have a business that serves the western region, regional players in the central or eastern states may be interested in growing their market share with a synergist purchase of your company. These buyers are competitors, so they are professionally qualified, but make sure that they have a strong balance sheet (a lot of cash and a small amount of debt). You should also be prepared that you will probably be asked to stay on in a management capacity to continue running the region after the merger. This is a big decision because if you sell and merge your business, you will become an employee of your own company!

## Acquire Undervalued Assets

At the writing of this book, we are experiencing the worst economy since the depression era. With so many businesses with declining revenues, there are bottom-feeding buyers with cash to burn and an appetite for acquisition. Be sure you are sitting down when you read their offer, but really, can you blame them? Don't throw in the towel just yet—if you are willing to participate in the financing and help grow the company back to profitability, there just might be a pot of gold at the end of the rainbow. I'll explain this more when we get to our discussion on "earnouts." Other items on a buyer's checklist to keep in mind:

- Earnings stability of the company over the last three to five years
- Gross profit margins
- Reputation of the brand in the marketplace
- Customer loyalty, turnover, and retention
- Customer diversity *vs.* concentration
- Personnel retention and depth of management team
- Market size and penetration rate
- Terms of the lease
- Condition of the equipment
- Verifiable books and records
- Appearance of the business and work areas
- Reasonable price expectations by the seller

## BROKER'S SECRET *GROWTH POTENTIAL*

Buyers will not pay for "growth potential." Buyers pay for past performance and buy for future potential. After all, if your business has so much growth potential, a buyer will wonder why you aren't doing those tasks yourself.

Now that you are well prepared with the perspective of your suitor, it's time to welcome that suitor into your business with a tour and day-in-the-life discussion of your operation.

## The Buyer, Seller, and Broker Meeting

The opportunity for you to sit down with a qualified buyer is the first reward of your hard efforts of preparing the business for sale and the broker's hard efforts in marketing to and attracting a qualified buyer.

All meetings with you and the buyer should be facilitated and attended by your broker.

The purpose of the first face-to-face meeting—or conference call if the buyer is out of the area—is to give the buyer a sense of the business and who you are as the owner. If you are calm, forthcoming with a reasonable amount of information, and accommodating, you will put the buyer at ease.

If you are defensive, resistant to the buyer's questions, and generally make the buyer feel uncomfortable, then you will most likely frighten your potential buyer away.

Buyers, whether they say it out loud or not, are frequently skeptical of a seller's presentation of the business because they fear that the seller is hiding problems in order to consummate the sale. If you are not successful at making the buyer feel comfortable right away, you will have to work much harder over the course of the transaction to constantly disprove all of the buyer's fears as they surface one by one.

With that said, a first meeting between the seller and buyer should not last more than two hours, so don't feel that you have to tell the suitor every single detail about the business since you wrote the start-up business plan. There should be a nice flow of questions and answers back and forth as well as a tour of the business if appropriate.

In order to maintain confidentiality with the employees, you may want to meet with the buyer after business hours, but don't be alarmed if you see the buyer sitting in a car across the street watching who comes and goes. It can be frustrating for a buyer if he or she is not able to visit the business when the employees are there and the business is operating, but you can't risk the word getting out, so stick to the plan and do not introduce the buyer to your employees until the deal is signed, sealed, and delivered.

Lastly, be prepared for an additional and possibly a third meeting with the buyer and even a conference call or two. After all, it's very difficult to lay hundreds of thousands or millions of dollars on the table if the buyer has only had one or two opportunities to visit a business. Try to understand that this is just the normal progression of a transaction and you would want the same courtesy if you were the buyer.

# Step Ten
## Secure an Offer

I am going to give you a very important broker's secret right out of the gate:

> ### BROKER'S SECRET *First Offer, Best Offer*
>
> Your first offer is often your best offer, and if it comes quickly after going to market, don't assume that it is because you priced the business too low. In fact, the business was probably priced just right, and savvy buyers know that they better not leave a profitable and well-priced business on the market because it will not be on the market for long!

So at this point you have met with the buyer multiple times, you may have answered what feels like 101 questions, and you are just about ready to say, "Never mind, I don't really want to sell after all!" At this juncture, try to remain steady, as this is the exact moment when the fun really begins because you have done the work and you have earned the golden ticket—the offer!

---

**BROKER'S SECRET** *CAUTIOUS OPTIMISM*

Offers are exciting but don't start counting your cash too soon because your deal isn't done until all of the closing documents are signed and the cash is in the bank.

---

An offer may come in different formats with many varied components. Below we will explore the most common so you will be comfortable when the time comes to review yours.

### Letter of Intent or Purchase Agreement

Many offers are initially presented in the form of a Letter of Intent, also called an LOI. LOIs are non-binding, but are an economical way for the buyer and seller to agree on the key terms of a deal before spending a lot of money on legal and accounting fees in the event that the parties are not in agreement.

If your business is priced below a million dollars, you may receive a formal purchase agreement right away. This agreement is binding once signed and returned, so consult your advisors before making your decision or writing a counter offer.

### Components of an Offer to Purchase

The components of an offer described below will be discussed as terms of a definitive or formal Asset Purchase Agreement but the same terms will often be included in an LOI or a Stock Purchase Agreement.

## The Price and Cash Due at Closing

All offers will begin with a paragraph that details what the total price, also called "consideration," will be.

If your business is priced reasonably for the market, you should expect an offer between 80 and 90 percent of your asking price. All buyers like to negotiate, so don't feel that this is their last offer. Before you accept or decline an offer, make sure you take into account all of the consideration contained in the deal such as interest on a promissory note or an employment agreement that may put thousands more in your pocket over time.

If your business is over-priced, you will most likely receive an offer between 50 and 80 percent of the asking price. In addition, the buyer will probably ask you to carry a note for a significant portion of the purchase price.

The offer will usually come with a 1 to 5 percent good faith deposit that will be fully refundable if the deal does not close prior to the buyer removing any contingencies (see Contingencies below) that are written into the offer.

In the price/consideration section of the offer, the terms for paying the balance of cash due less the deposit will be described. The terms may be all cash, cash plus a promissory note issued by the seller, cash plus third-party financing from a lender, or a blend of all three. Occasionally, assumption of existing business debt will be included as consideration.

## Seller Financing or Promissory Note

As discussed in Step Three, a typical seller's note will be between 10 percent on the low end to 50 percent on the high end of the offering price. The size of the note will tend to be more if the business is a service-related company with little to no tangible assets such as equipment and inventory.

The note will usually be personally guaranteed by the buyer and secured by the assets of the business.

The note offered as part of the consideration will also detail the interest that will be paid on the principal and the number of months or years that it will be paid.

If the buyer is also securing bank or third-party financing to close the deal, be prepared that your note will be subordinated to the bank's loan, meaning that if the buyer defaults, the bank gets all of its money before you get a single penny.

## Third-Party Financing

In a deal where the buyer offers consideration in the form of a down payment and third-party financing, up to 80 percent of the cash paid to you at closing will come from a loan secured by the buyer to purchase your business.

The good news is that the cash received from the lender to the buyer, is all cash to you. The bad news is that lenders will require your buyer to jump over many hurdles before they approve the loan, so plan on a sixty- to ninety-day closing.

## Earnout

Earnouts are a financing structure often used with service businesses, professional medical practices, and businesses that are heavily dependent on the seller. With an earnout, a portion of the purchase price is paid over time like a promissory note; however, the payments are not fixed. Payments are usually structured as a percentage of gross revenues or gross margin, payable monthly, quarterly, or annually for a specific term. An earnout gives buyers comfort in knowing that they will only have to pay the seller if current customers remain in place. If the customers leave after the sale, buyers will only pay for the remaining clients protecting them from attrition due to change of ownership.

While this is an excellent strategy for a buyer, sellers are not as comfortable with earnouts because they no longer have control over the operation of the business after the sale. However, an earnout is an ideal structure if your business is seller-dependent or if your revenues have declined but you anticipate steady or rapid future growth.

## BROKER'S SECRET *EARNOUTS*

An earnout clause should be crafted and reviewed by very experienced attorneys on behalf of both parties. Because of possible ambiguities about payments, conflicts may arise requiring formal dispute resolution, so a clearly written and agreed upon clause will serve all parties well in the long run.

### Assumption of Debt

If a business is on the market with liabilities on the balance sheet, a savvy buyer may reduce the purchase price and subsequently the cash down payment by assuming the liabilities on the books. This is most likely to occur with a stock sale in which a buyer is essentially purchasing all asset and liabilities on the balance sheet.

## BROKER'S SECRET *COUNTER OFFERS*

Never reject an offer—always make a counter offer. The buyer's first offer is usually to set a baseline for the negotiation, so don't be offended, just counter back. Once a dialogue begins between you and the buyer, the goal will be to agree somewhere in the middle that feels like a win-win for both parties.

## Assets Included in the Deal

The second paragraph usually details which assets are included in the deal. The assets typically included are any and all other assets presently used in the business including trade name(s), phone and fax numbers, software licenses, domain name(s), Marketing materials, customer list, website(s) and related data and information, copies of books and records, client relationships, client contracts, databases, all intellectual property, leaseholds, equipment, fixtures, franchise agreements, licenses, goodwill, proprietary information, and non-compete agreements with seller and seller's partners.

Not included unless the transaction is a stock sale are cash, deposits, or bank accounts.

Receivables, payables, inventory, and working capital can be paid for in cash by the buyer or included in the sale. Oftentimes, these items are negotiated between buyer and seller on an item-by-item basis.

## Non-Compete Clause

Remember our discussion on your motivation to sell and having a clear vision about how you will spend your time or make additional income after the sale? Your true motivation will be tested with the Non-Competition or Non-Compete Clause. This is where the buyer will contractually prevent you from operating a similar business or consulting with a similar business for three to ten years within the geographic range of the existing customer base. If you are not willing to agree to a reasonable Non-Compete, you will not be able to sell your business.

## Consulting Income or Employment Agreement

Consulting or Employment Agreements are an excellent strategy to move consideration outside of the purchase agreement to potentially reduce taxes for the seller, provide a tax write-off after the sale for the buyer, and further ensure the buyer that the seller will remain after the sale to assist with the transition and retention of employees and clients.

Consulting and employment agreements can be as short as three months and as long as multiple years, depending on the desires of the parties.

## Contingencies

Contingencies will be written into your offer to ensure that the buyer will have adequate time, information, and financing to determine if the buyer is going to consummate the deal.

Contingencies are a critical part of your transaction. Deals live or die based on the seller's ability to provide information that will allow the buyer to confidently remove all of the contingencies.

Typical contingencies include the following:

1. Due diligence or review of financial documents and records

2. Buyer's approval for third-party financing

3. Buyer's approval by the landlord for lease assignment or new lease

4. Buyer's approval of licensing requirements

5. Buyer's franchise approval

6. Clearance on environmental issues if real estate is included

## Due Diligence

Due diligence is the period of time in a transaction in which both the buyer and the seller have the opportunity to investigate the other party. The goal is to investigate to the extent required to allow the buyer to make an informed decision about the business's ability to continue and the buyer's ability to operate after the sale. Due to the importance and complexity of the due diligence process, we will discuss it in greater detail in Step Nine.

## Approval of Third-Party Financing

Financing will always be a contingency to the transaction if the buyer will require proceeds beyond the buyer's cash and seller's note or earnout.

If a buyer is unable to receive approval from a lender or the terms of the available loan are not acceptable to the buyer, the buyer has the right to reject the loan and withdraw the offer.

## Lease Assignment

As we previously discussed, lease assignment can be a deal killer. I can't stress this enough: make sure you and your broker understand the requirements of the landlord in order to assign your facilities lease to a new buyer. In addition, the lease must have a sufficient term remaining or be negotiated prior to going to market in order for the buyer to meet a lender's lease requirements. A lender will only lend if the lease in place is equal or greater to the term of the loan, so the landlord must accept the qualifications of the buyer and extend a lease term acceptable to both the buyer and their bank. Most SBA loans for businesses are for ten years, so the new lease can be for five years with one five-year option or any reasonable combination thereof.

Even if a lender is not involved, landlords can be very particular about who they will transfer a lease to, so make sure that when the buyer meets the landlord, you or your broker have "packaged" your buyer with a résumé, credit report, and personal tax returns that will address the landlords concerns up front.

Also remember that your landlord probably will not relieve you of financial responsibility for the existing term of the lease with the assignment to the buyer. A landlord will most often keep you in back-up position to the buyer should your buyer default on the rent. If you are carrying a note, you have already agreed to remain involved in the business (you can watch your investment that way), so this may not be a major issue. However, if you receive all cash for the business and have the ability to walk away after the transition period, you may be disheartened by remaining financially responsible for the lease. The bottom line is to secure the most qualified buyer that you can find in order to increase the likelihood that your landlord may consider absolving you completely from any future liability.

## Licensing Requirements

If there are critical licenses to generate revenue for the business such as an Alcoholic Beverage (ABC) License, the ability of the buyer to obtain the license might be a contingency of the sale and delay the closing until the license has been secured. Other licenses such as a Contractor's License may not be a contingency if the seller agrees to allow the buyer to operate under their license for a period of time. This can be risky for the seller in the event that any liabilities remain with the license holder or that the buyer may not be able to qualify for the license. The type of license and the qualifications of the buyer will determine your comfort level with how to manage a license contingency.

## Franchise Approval

If your business is a franchise, the franchisor will always have the first right of refusal to buy your franchise without allowing you to place your business on the open market. If the franchisor is not interested in purchasing your unit, the franchisor will reserve the right to approve all potential buyers.

In addition, you will not be able to close your escrow until your buyer has completed franchisee training. Franchisee training can be as short as one week and as long as several months. Regardless of the length of training, you will not be able to close your escrow until training has been successfully completed in the event the buyer does not pass the training.

## Clearance on Environmental Issues

If you are selling your building along with the business and a lender will provide financing, environmental clearance in the form of a report called a Phase I will be a contingency. This report will disclose to all parties that the soil under the building is not contaminated and does not require further testing or remediation (removal of contaminated soil). In the event of a negative Phase I report, a Phase II will be required which will create expenses and delays that will need to be agreed upon by all parties before proceeding.

## Buyer and Seller Representations and Warranties

Representations and Warranties are the critical catchall section of the agreement that make promises to the buyer and the seller that there are no misrepresentations, no outstanding liens or encumbrances, and that the business is in compliance with any and all local, state, and federal regulations and agencies. The buyer is generally warranting the ability to perform or fully execute the agreement. Representations and Warranties can be a few sentences, paragraphs, or multiple pages depending on the price of the company.

## Allocation of Purchase Price

The Allocation of the Purchase Price can often be a secondary negotiation in a multi-million-dollar deal where tax mitigation is a significant driver in the transaction. The allocation declares for the Internal Revenue Service how the consideration paid in the sale will be allocated for tax purposes. For example, if the sale price is $1,000,000, a simple allocation might look like this (*for illustrative purposes only*):

ABC Company

ALLOCATION OF THE PURCHASE PRICE

| | |
|---|---|
| Purchase Price: | $1,000,000 |
| Inventory: | $100,000 |
| Furniture Fixtures & Equipment: | $50,000 |
| Lease Assignment: | $10,000 |
| Leasehold Improvements: | $50,000 |
| Covenant Not to Compete: | $100,000 |
| Goodwill: | $690,000 |
| Total | $1,000,000 |

The allocation is usually prepared by each party's transaction accountant and is presented to the other side for acceptance or negotiation. The manner in which consideration is allocated can reduce the taxes paid by the buyer or the seller significantly depending on how items are allocated to be taxed as a capital gain, ordinary income, or a deductible expense in the year incurred. The Allocation of the Purchase Price should be addressed early in the overall negotiations so as not to become a deal breaker just when you thought that the deal was done.

## BROKER'S SECRET *PURCHASE PRICE ALLOCATION*

The Allocation of the Purchase Price for the seller must match the allocation for the buyer *exactly*, without exception.

### Training and Transition

Depending on the size of the deal, a buyer will negotiate a certain amount of training and transition time by you personally and possibly a key employee at no cost to the buyer after the closing.

The training period at no cost can be from two weeks to four weeks depending on the complexity of the business. After four weeks, you should negotiate a consulting agreement clearly detailing your hourly rate and the expected number of hours committed to on a weekly basis.

If you are carrying a promissory note or have an earnout, you should err on the generous side with your time to ensure the buyer's success and increase the likelihood of receiving on-time payments on your outstanding note.

## Desired Closing Date

This is the finish line! If you are in a position to review multiple offers and the price, terms, and buyer qualifications are similar, the closing date may become a deciding factor. When determining your acceptable closing date, be certain to take into consideration the due diligence period, the time it takes to remove a loan contingency, and the tax advantages of closing in the current year or not.

## Dispute Resolution

No buyer or seller wants to anticipate the worst; however, all agreements must have a dispute resolution clause. Most agreements require mediation before binding arbitration in the event of a dispute between parties. Discuss your clause with your advisors taking into consideration the laws of your state.

## Expiration Date

The seller's response date on the offer is also called the expiration date. All Letters of Intent and Purchase Agreements will have an expiration date, which should be acknowledged and adhered to. If a seller or buyer does not respond by the dates detailed in the agreement, the agreement may expire and possibly result in a loss of deposit by the buyer or cause the seller to incur costs. Time is always of the essence and dates are included in the contract for a reason!

## Handling Multiple Offers

Your reward for building a highly profitable business in a highly desirable industry will come in the form of multiple offers.

Multiple offers should be managed by your broker in an ethical and swift manner in order to keep all parties interested and fairly notified of the status of their offer.

As a seller, you may decide to accept an offer of one or more of the suitors contingent on the swift completion of due diligence or you may choose to counter offer all potential buyers in hopes that one or more suitors will increase the offer to secure "first position." It will be to your advantage to place the remaining buyers in back-up positions in the event that the selected buyer is unable to resolve contingencies.

Handling multiple offers will require the skills of an experienced business broker to ensure that you have all the information necessary for you to select the best offer—which ultimately may or may not be based on the highest price.

Once you have successfully completed your negotiation and an offer has been accepted, the next step will be for your buyer to complete a more in-depth investigation of your business, commonly known as the due diligence period.

Once a buyer has satisfactorily completed due diligence, you will be a giant step closer to closing, so now is the time to hold your breath and cross your fingers...

# Step Eleven
## Due Diligence

Due diligence, after closing the deal, is the most exciting time in a transaction! This is the time when all of your painstakingly detailed preparation validates for the buyer that in fact your business really is the dream business the buyer has been searching for.

For many sellers, due diligence can be a very nerve-wracking and vulnerable time, but only if you have not adequately prepared and openly disclosed any issues related to your business.

> ## BROKER'S SECRET *BUSINESS SKELETONS*
>
> Due diligence is not a time for surprises. Every business has a skeleton or two, so share any problems with your broker and the buyer right away. If you reveal your concerns early in the process, you will hopefully have time to resolve the issues. However, if you wait until due diligence, that small little skeleton may suddenly become frightening enough to scare your buyer away.

To further understand and prepare for the buyer's list of documents to review, we will now discuss the most frequently requested items. Keep in mind that each buyer's list will be different; some will be fairly short and others will be very long and very detailed.

## Previous Three Years of Historical Financial Statements

You will be asked to provide at minimum the previous three years of profit and loss statements and year-end balance sheets. You may also be asked to provide monthly P&Ls for year-to-date and the previous twelve months. This will allow a buyer to see how income and expenses flow through the business.

## Previous Three Years of Tax Returns

Provide copies of all pages from your federal tax returns (not your state or personal returns) including all schedules.

## List of Employees

The list should include all employee names, positions, how long they have been with the company, and a few sentences about their duties. If you are having challenges with an employee or are concerned that a key employee may leave, be sure to share your concerns with the buyer to avoid problems later.

## Customer Lists

Although the buyer has signed a confidentiality agreement, you may feel uncomfortable releasing the names of your customers to the buyer at this stage. Since the buyer needs to review every account and the revenue generated by each, you may consider providing a list of customers with only their account numbers at the early stages of due diligence. If all goes well with financing and lease approval by the landlord, you can provide a second customer list with names revealed. Transparency is critical, but incremental sharing is perfectly acceptable.

## Accounts Receivable Aging Report

This should be a current Aging Report for the buyer to review. Be prepared to discuss the credit terms you offer your customers and any accounts over sixty days. A buyer will use this information when determining how much they will pay or "credit" you for receivables on the books, so understand your report in detail and be prepared to discuss each account individually.

## Facility Lease

Provide a complete copy of your lease. If your lease will expire soon, remember to have a lease proposal from your landlord available for your buyer to review as well.

## Equipment Leases

Most buyers will want to assume leases for equipment that is used to operate the business. This includes small items such credit card machines, alarm, and telephone systems to large items such as heaving operating equipment. This also includes vehicle leases. Provide copies of all leases and understand in advance the requirements for transfer and assignment.

## Licenses

If your business requires a license to operate, such as an Alcoholic Beverage license (ABC License,) a buyer will need to apply for and be approved by that agency to operate the business. Understand the necessary licensing transfer steps and fees as well as the timeframe required. Brokers should also be able to provide you with insight based on their direct experience with licensing agencies.

## Franchise Agreement

If your business is a franchise, you should re-read your franchise agreement, particularly the section on transferring your unit before you put your business on the market. All franchisors have a process for selling an individual unit and most reserve "first right of refusal" to buy the unit back before allowing you to sell to a third party. If the franshisor decides to waive its right to purchase, it will still have final approval of the buyer so understand clearly what the requirements are before entertaining an offer. Also, be sure to provide your buyer with a list detailing all of the upfront costs of purchasing the franchise such as the transfer fee, the training fee, upgrade requirements, the lease deposit, and working capital over and above the cash down payment. Often at the time of sale, a franshisor will require the franchisee or potential buyer to implement any new signage or marketing programs that you may have resisted, so the party responsible for payment of the possibly six-figure upgrades should be addressed and detailed in the offer.

## Environmental Reports

If the real estate is being sold, the lender will require an environmental report disclosing any potential contamination in the soil before approving a loan. With the sale of a food business, a health inspection may be required prior to final transfer of ownership. Be sure to provide copies of all licenses and clearances including their expiration dates for the buyer's examination.

## Pension, Profit-Sharing, and Miscellaneous Employee Benefit Plans

Provide copies of all plans that the buyer will be expected to continue on behalf of the employees after the sale. It is not reasonable to think that benefits and incentive plans can be removed after a sale to increase the profitability of the company. A buyer may risk losing key employees if he or she changes the benefit plan, so the buyer needs to understand obligations to the employees thoroughly.

## Union Contracts or Organization Activity

If your business is unionized, be sure that you have a transaction attorney on your success team who specializes in the sale of unionized companies. Like all other agreements, provide a complete copy of your current union contract(s) for the buyer's review.

## Insurance Policies

Buyers will be required to apply for their own policies (unless your deal is a stock sale) but will usually remain with the existing provider for the first year to expedite processing. You will not be able to assign your policy, but you will be reimbursed on a pro-rated basis for any premium that you paid in advance.

## Pending or Threatened Litigation

If you have been sued within the last ten years or anticipate being involved in litigation with a customer, employee, vendor, or any other party in relation to the company, you must disclose it to the buyer. This is a deal breaker! In an asset sale, no liabilities will transfer to the buyer so the buyer will be protected, and in a stock sale, the seller can fully indemnify the buyer. Either way, litigation is frightening to a buyer but if disclosed early with clear protections, the sale of your company will still have the ability to move forward.

## Corporate Minutes

If the business is incorporated, all material changes that have occurred within the business should have been recorded in the Corporate Minutes. By reviewing the minutes, the buyer will have a documented history of the company's activity providing a chronological operational history of the business.

> ## BROKER'S SECRET *CORPORATE MINUTES*
>
> Make sure your corporate minutes are current before placing your business on the market, particularly in the event of a stock sale as they will reviewed in detail during due diligence.

## Disclosure Statement

If you are working with a broker, you will be required to complete a Seller and Buyer Disclosure Statement (buyers complete their portion when they submit an offer). I can't begin to tell you how important this document is to both parties. Through first-hand experience, in the event of a dispute, this statement is one of the first documents reviewed by representatives for each party.

The Seller and Buyer's Disclosure Statement provided to you by your broker will ask you all of the critical questions to trigger items that you should share with a buyer before they become an issue in due diligence or worse, after the sale.

When completing the statement, take time to honestly and thoroughly respond to every question. It's also a good idea to review your answers from a buyer's perspective. Would you feel comfortable buying your business? Even if a question requires you to state facts that may make a buyer uncomfortable, by doing so up front, you have given yourself the time to prepare an honest explanation as to why you answered the question in the manner that you did.

The Seller and Buyer's Disclosure is not a document to fear, but rather a document to respect as your responses to the questions may be the difference between a sale or not—or in the worst-case scenario a trip to the courtroom or not.

## BROKER'S SECRET *Disclosure Statement*

If your broker doesn't require you to complete a disclosure statement, get a new broker! This document, if completed honestly and updated if there are any material changes, will keep you out of court. Even if you somehow end up in a dispute, presenting your disclosure statement will probably save you thousands of dollars so NEVER skip this step!

### Seller's Due Diligence

As the seller and possible financier of the sale, you have the right to conduct due diligences as well.

Your experienced broker will have already provided you with the buyer's résumé or biography statement and the buyer's personal financial statement.

If the buyer's offer requests seller financing, you should ask to review the following documents:

1. **Proof of Down Payment**
   The buyer should provide you with a bank statement that shows adequate cash to cover the down payment and three months working capital. If the lender is providing funding, the lender will require the buyer to add working capital to the new loan, so less personal cash on hand by the buyer is acceptable.

2. **Buyer's Credit Report**
   The buyer can order an official credit report online to provide for your review. A buyer with a credit score below 700 but adequate cash to close the deal should provide an explanation to you if you are financing more than 20 percent of the sale. After all, a bank will require the same justification and since you are acting as a bank, it is within your right to ask. Based on the information received, discuss the buyer's response with your success team and determine if any identified risks outweigh the rewards of selling to that particular buyer.

3. **Tax Returns**
   You can request to review a buyer's personal federal tax returns for the previous three years. The purpose of your review is to determine if the buyer has a solid income history and if they have a second source of income. A second income can be critical to ensure that a buyer's personal expenses are covered so the buyer is not tempted to deplete resources from the business to pay for personal expenses.

**BROKER'S SECRET** *IDENTITY THEFT*

Ask the buyer to black out social security numbers on his or her credit report and tax returns before providing them to you. Your broker should do the same for your tax returns. In a time when identity theft is rampant, you can never be too careful.

Once all initial due diligence documents have been exchanged, be prepared for a few more face-to-face meetings and requests for additional documents.

A buyer should not have personal discussions with your key employees or customers unless the employees or customers already know that your business is on the market. Some buyers will insist on participating in meetings involving employees or customers, so you may be forced to think of a creative way to introduce the buyer to your team without exposing the sale. However, be prepared that employees and customers don't like surprises either and if they later learn that a "consultant" was actually a buyer, ill will may be created, so proceed carefully with satisfying the buyer but protecting your most valuable assets—your employees and your customers.

### Definitive Purchase Agreement

If your deal has been negotiated based on a Letter of Intent, the definitive (final) purchase agreement will be prepared and negotiated during due diligence. The LOI should have addressed all critical elements of the agreement, so the definitive agreement should not be a time for surprises and delays.

A purchase agreement can be as short as a few pages or as long as twenty plus pages depending on the size of the deal and the complexity of the deal structure. To have a better understanding of the type of agreement that your broker or attorney will prepare, ask for a sample at the beginning of due diligence so you can educate yourself in advance of the final hour.

## Conclusion of Due Diligence

If all goes well, due diligence should conclude between twenty-one and forty-five days after the initial Letter of Intent of Purchase Agreement.

At the conclusion, all contingencies should be removed in writing including the following:

1. Verification and Acceptance of Financial Performance

2. Approval of Third-Party Financing

3. Approval of Lease Assignment

4. Allocation of the Purchase Price

Concluding contingencies may possibly include the following as well:

1. Franchise Approval

2. License Transfer

3. Environmental Clearance

4. Any Other Contingencies Written into the
   Agreement

Once all contingencies have been removed in writing, you are in the home stretch and the closing process can be begin!

# Step Twelve

## Close the Deal and Exit Smoothly

Once you get to the closing stage, all items have been negotiated, the paperwork is complete, and all that is remaining
is the closing!

Depending on your state, the closing or final legal transfer of your business will be processed by an escrow company that handles bulk sale escrows or an attorney who is
experienced in business closings.

A bulk sale escrow is required in many states whenever a
business sells more than 51 percent of its inventory. A bulk
sale escrow is not required with a stock sale. Check with
your broker or attorney regarding the bulk sale requirements in your state.

Regardless of bulk sale, the following closing documents
are prepared on behalf of the seller and buyer:

1. Escrow or Closing Instructions
2. Bill of Sale
3. Covenant Not to Compete
4. Settlement Sheet Consideration and Expense
   Proration
5. UCC-1 Security Filing and Recording for Loans
   and Promissory Notes

6. Lien Search and Clearance on the Business
7. Creditor Settlements
8. Closing Document Storage

## Escrow or Closing Instructions

Escrow or Closing Instructions is a boilerplate document that "instructs" the escrow or closing officer regarding the who, what, where, why, when, and how of the transaction. Upon opening escrow, initial instructions are prepared and shared with the buyer and seller for written approval. Once the escrow process is complete, final instructions will be issued and signed immediately before the closing.

## Bill of Sale

The Bill of Sale is usually a one-page document that is essentially a receipt or proof of the sale detailing the parties, the date, the location, and the amount of consideration paid.

## Covenant to Not Compete

The Covenant to Not Compete or Non-Competition has a value assigned to it from the Allocation of the Purchase Price, so a separate one-page statement is created specifically for the covenant. This page also acts as a receipt and details the specific terms of the covenant.

## Settlement Sheet

The Settlement Sheet is often the cover sheet to the Escrow Instructions detailing the debits and credits to the buy side and to the sell side. The debits are usually for the escrow or closing fees, administrative costs, franchise fees, creditors paid in escrow, brokers fees, and pro-rated expenses for either side.

Credits are usually the cash placed in escrow by the buyer and or lender or credits to a buyer for inventory, receivables, or other agreed upon items.

There is typically a separate settlement sheet for the buyer and for the seller as their debits and credits will be different based on decisions made regarding which party will pay which fees.

## Cash Management

Escrow or your attorney's trust account will handle all collection and disbursement of cash. In the event of a dispute, all parties (seller, buyer, and the broker) must sign to release funds, so funds placed in escrow are always a very positive sign that the transaction is moving and is closer to closing.

## UCC-1 Security Agreement Filing and Recording for Loans and Promissory Notes

A UCC-1 Security Agreement is the official recording instrument within the county of operation that advises that there is a lien on the business assets and/or real estate as collateral for a bank loan or a promissory note. The lien is recorded to notify any purchaser in the event that the buyer attempts to sell the business (assets) before the loans are paid off.

## Lien Search and Clearance

The lien search and clearance is one of the most important aspects of a bulk sale or business escrow. During a bulk sale process, a notice is placed in a local newspaper for a certain number of business days, usually ten, to notify any creditors that the assets are being sold. This notification process includes all taxing agencies such as the Internal Revenue Service and the state taxing authorities who will be notified directly.

Any outstanding taxes, liens, or miscellaneous debts will be identified and given the opportunity to be presented to escrow with a demand for payment. The escrow officer or attorney will receive approval from the seller to settle or pay all outstanding debts or the escrow will not be able to close. Your escrow will not be able to close until all claims in escrow are settled, regardless of how small or how large.

In addition to paying off all debt prior to the closing, by going through the bulk sale process, a buyer will be relieved of all "successor liability" and any creditors who do not place a claim in escrow during the allowable time period will not be able to pursue the buyer for payments owed by the seller prior to change of ownership.

## BROKER'S SECRET >>> *SUCCESSOR LIABILITY*

If you grow your business by acquiring assets from another company, do not buy the assets without a lien clearance. Successor liability for unknown back taxes, debts, or litigation can bankrupt you!

## Creditor Settlements

Your escrow officer or closing attorney will be responsible for dispersing all fees and settlements due to claimants from the proceeds of your sale, so the good news is that any dollars owed will not have to come out of your pocket prior to the closing.

## Closing Document Storage

Closing documents will usually be stored on your behalf for approximately three years depending on your state's requirements. However, both buyer and seller should maintain their own copies of the closing documents in their permanent records.

## Stock Sale Closing Documents

If your sale is a stock sale, many of the same documents will be prepared for your transaction, plus several others that allow for the corporations' shares to be sold to another shareholder.

In addition, the current shareholders and officers (most likely the seller) will have to officially resign and the new shareholders and officers (most likely the buyer) will have to be elected. These documents will all become a part of the existing Corporate Minutes that will have been purchased by the buyer. With a stock sale, a bulk sale is not required as all asset and liabilities are included; however, most buyers will want to conduct a lien search to uncover any liabilities that may have inadvertently not been disclosed during due diligence.

## Cash Me Out!

Congratulations! The day you have been waiting for has finally arrived...payday!

After months of preparation, participation, and perspiration you have made it. Your final proceeds will be wired to your account directly from escrow or trust. Your wealth manager should be standing by to diversify your new cash position and your travel agent is right next to her with your tickets to an exotic location of your dreams. But wait! There is one last step required before you board the plane—the transition and training period.

## Transition from Seller to Buyer

I am not going to sugarcoat this. The transition and training period can be a very tense time, first for the seller and then for the buyer.

During the beginning of the transition, you are elated to have received an amazing amount of money for all of your years of hard work and exit planning, but soon after closing, reality begins to set in.

You have just sold your business, and the new owner is beyond excited about taking over the helm. In your opinion, however, the new owner isn't running the business in the same perfect way that you ran it. But don't worry. You have the cash, and the new owner probably owes you more money, so take a deep breath and teach the buyer in the best and most patient way you can how to make that business hum!

Now it's the buyer's turn. When the buyer first bought the business, he or she secretly planned to add his or her own magic to make it even more successful than it was the day he or she took over. But after a couple of weeks, the new owner begins to realize that it's tough to teach an old business new tricks! The buyer's honeymoon is now over. Reality has set in that the buyer has a big loan payment to make for the next 120 months, and fears about what to do if the sales drop for some unknown reason become a frequent nightmare.

Sounds scary, but again, don't worry. This is a natural transition process and if you anticipate it, it won't sting quite as badly.

Smooth transitions come from detailed advanced planning, patience, and an open mind on the seller's part. Plan to transition the business to the buyer as if you were leaving a very trusted and respected manager to run your business while you were away for a yearlong dream vacation.

Review and introduce each account to the buyer, especially the top ten customers.

Help the buyer connect with each employee, but give them space to create a fresh dynamic as the new owner.

Create operational checklists for each department to make it easy for the buyer to reference late at night when he or she is the last one there and can't remember what the alarm code is.

And lastly, create an environment for lasting success. The legacy of your business is not your responsibility, but it's an added feather in your cap if your company can continue to grow and thrive without you. It's probably the ultimate compliment—not to mention it's the only way your promissory note will get paid off!

Now that your transition period is complete, you are *finally free!*

Free to jump with both feet into the next phase of your life or simply to wake up each morning and revel in the fact that you get to do as much of nothing that day as you want to.

Either way, you did it!

You built an enterprise worthy of being desired by someone else and you have gracefully and professionally *exited your business receiving the price you deserve!*

Congratulations!

# Epilogue

You now have *more* than enough information to make your exit dreams come true, but will you take advantage of the treasure chest of tools in the next section of the book and start your exit journey now?

Working on your exit journey immediately will not only add value for the future, it will also add value for you financially and mentally *today* as you re-energize around your new vision of financial freedom. If you don't start thinking about your plan today, what will your options be in three, four, or five years from now?

As a transaction expert, I am very aware of how overwhelming this task can be. However, I have simplified the selling process to make your future sale as easy as reading the checklist, visualizing your plan, and then start committing dates to paper.

One of my most satisfying transactions was facilitating the sale of a $5 million company that had perfect financial statements and was ready for market when we listed. They owners had begun three years earlier getting the right employees in place, diversifying the customer list, and eliminating unnecessary owner benefits from the financial statements.

When we went to market, within three months we had multiple buyers, which allowed the sellers to choose the most professionally and financially qualified buyer to take over their company. As a result of the seller's knowledge of the process and advance planning, the buyer was able to secure the highest amount of bank financing available, resulting in the business owner's ability to cash out with the ultimate price they deserved.

This is a true story and my next favorite story could be yours! You chose this book because you are ready to start your exit journey and position your company for the very highest price, just like the sellers in my favorite story did.

Now all you have to do is turn the page and start working on the checklist...today!

For additional support and inspiration to achieve your exit goals, visit www.exitjourney.com for more tools, tips, and videos to further ensure that you sell your company for the highest price and fund the dreams in the next phase of your life.

# WRAPPING
# IT
# ALL
# UP

"For everyone that succeeds, it's because there's somebody there to show you the way out."
~Oprah Winfrey, CEO, HARPO Companies, Inc.

# Checklist to Sell Your Business for the Price You Deserve

- ❑ Plan for the sale
- ❑ Have a legitimate reason for selling
- ❑ Sell when your industry is hot
- ❑ Sell when interest rates for borrowing are low
- ❑ Sell when business buyers are plentiful
- ❑ Sell when your business has been profitable for three years
- ❑ Know the value of your business at any given time
- ❑ Go to market with a clear pricing strategy
- ❑ Pre-qualify your business for financing
- ❑ Pre-negotiate an advantageous lease with your landlord
- ❑ Gather all selling documents in one location
- ❑ Record all sales and expenses on your P&Ls
- ❑ Eliminate co-mingling of business and personal assets
- ❑ Eliminate marginal owner perks paid by the business
- ❑ Comply with all tax authorities
- ❑ Scrub the balance sheet of old liabilities or assets
- ❑ Do your own due diligence as if you were a buyer
- ❑ Engage an experience business broker or intermediary
- ❑ Engage a tax accountant
- ❑ Engage a wealth manager or financial planner
- ❑ Engage a transaction attorney
- ❑ Identify an SBA preferred business lender

- ❑ Determine if "For Sale by Owner" is a viable option
- ❑ Determine if you should sell assets or stock
- ❑ Prepare marketing documents such as a Confidential Business Review or Investment Summary
- ❑ Understand why a buyer would buy your type of business
- ❑ Understand the components of a Letter of Intent or Purchase Agreement including
    - ○ Price and cash due at closing
    - ○ Financing via seller note, third party, or earnout
    - ○ Assets and/or liabilities included in the deal
    - ○ Non-compete clause
    - ○ Consulting or employment agreements
    - ○ Contingencies to closing
    - ○ Due diligence term and required items for review
    - ○ Lease approval and assignment
    - ○ License approvals and/or transfers
    - ○ Franchise approval
    - ○ Representations and warranties
    - ○ Allocation of the purchase price
    - ○ Training and transition period
    - ○ Desired closing date
    - ○ Dispute resolution
    - ○ Expiration of the offer
- ❑ Manage the buyer and seller due diligence process
- ❑ Execute the definitive purchase agreement
- ❑ Sign escrow and/or closing documents
- ❑ Transition period from seller to buyer
- ❑ Done!

# Broker's Secrets

### Broker's Secret >>> Competitor Calling
When a competitor calls, proceed with extreme caution due to confidentiality and never share ANY information with a competitor without expert advice from a business broker, transaction attorney, and/or an accountant.

### Broker's Secret >>> Legacy vs. Cash
Selling to a third party almost always results in a higher price and better terms, but if you decide to sell to your family, I both respect and applaud you. Remember to do your tax planning and take a lot of pictures the day you hand over the keys.

### Broker's Secret >>> No Financing, No Deal!
If your business's tax returns don't qualify for traditional bank financing, your business may not be sellable, and the only banker left will be the "Bank of First National Seller" (YOU), which is definitely not going to be your first choice.

### Broker's Secret >>> Corporate Parachuters
Ex-corporate middle managers look great on paper, present well, and have large 401(k)s to secure financing, but they are used to spending other people's money. When it comes time to reach into their own pockets, they may not be able to pull the trigger. Ask questions to uncover their risk tolerance such as, "Were your parents entrepreneurs?" so you don't waste time with someone who will never go all the way to the finish line.

### Broker's Secret >>> The 1x Myth

Contrary to popular belief, a business is rarely valued at 1 times revenue! Don't have your business valued by your accountant (unless they are accredited in business valuation) or your attorney. They may not have access to market comparables (comps) or an understanding of how the business-for-sale market is currently trading.

### Broker's Secret >>> Customer Concentration

Customer concentration is a deal killer. Diversify immediately or postpone your sale. You probably won't be able to sell anyway and you definitely won't receive the maximum price for your company.

### Broker's Secret >>> Asking vs. Selling

When researching comparables currently being advertised, remember that the asking price is not the final selling price, so don't set false pricing expectations for your business based on someone else's false expectations.

### Broker's Secret >>> Family on the Payroll

Non-working family members on the payroll is cash to the bottom line and they don't need to be replaced/adjusted for. Just be sure that you can prove to your potential buyer that they truly don't work in the business or add value to the business whatsoever.

### Broker's Secret >>> BOEV Formula

A formula this valuable bears repeating....

Profit + Owner Benefits + Depreciation + Amortization
+ Interest = (SDE) x 2x to 4x Multiple =
Fair Market Price Range

### Broker's Secret >>> Pricing Strategy

Your debts or your retirement income needs are not a buyer's concern and should not be a significant factor when determining your pricing strategy.

### Broker's Secret >>> Growth is Good

Declining revenue is a deal killer! If you have a large one-time expense such as a large equipment purchase, the bank may allow you to add that income back to your Seller's Discretionary Earnings, but be prepared for an uphill battle. Banks like flat or growing sales so monitor your Profit and Loss Statements on a monthly basis at minimum.

### Broker's Secret >>> Landlords

Landlords arc deal killers, too! Many business owners don't want to advise the landlord that they are selling the business which is a major mistake. The statement "approval will not unreasonably be withheld" is written into 99 percent of all of the commercial leases. The only thing they don't tell you is that they can be so unreasonable with their terms that the buyer may reject the landlord AND your business! Be brave; notify the landlord of your intentions before you go to market so at least you can deal with any potential roadblocks before they become insurmountable.

### Broker's Secret >>> Stock Warning!

Business owners, do not try this on your own! Speak to an experienced advisor before attempting to sell stock!

### Broker's Secret >>> Tax Mitigation

Your experienced transaction accountant and transaction attorney will counsel you on tax-saving deal strategies such as allocating a portion of the proceeds to employment and/ or consulting agreements, personal goodwill, and other tax management strategies which will more than pay for their fees.

### Broker's Secret >>> Broker Cooperation
Business brokers, unlike real estate agents, do not have an official Multiple Listing Service (MLS) and do not automatically "cooperate" or "co-broker," meaning share fees, with other business brokers. The reason stated is usually based on protecting confidentiality, which can be a valid reason, but this is an important strategy to discuss with your broker. You should ask your broker directly, "Do you cooperate with other brokers?" If the answer is no, you should ask why and also know that it is within your right to request that they do.

### Broker's Secret >>> Multiple Offers
Unlike buyers for a house, it is very unlikely that you will have multiple offers for your business unless it is very profitable with very clean books in a growing industry.

### Broker's Secret >>> Growth Potential
Buyers will not pay for "growth potential." Buyers pay for past performance and buy for future potential. After all, if your business has so much growth potential, a buyer will wonder why you aren't doing those tasks yourself.

### Broker's Secret >>> First Offer, Best Offer
Your first offer is often your best offer, and if it comes quickly after going to market, don't assume that it is because you priced the business too low. In fact, the business was probably priced just right and savvy buyers know that they better not leave a profitable and well-priced business on the market because it will not be on the market for long!

### Broker's Secret >>> Cautious Optimism

Offers are exciting, but don't start counting your cash too soon because your deal isn't done until all of the closing documents are signed and the cash is in the bank.

### Broker's Secret >>> Earnouts

An earnout clause should be crafted and reviewed by very experienced attorneys on behalf of both parties. Because of possible ambiguities about payments, conflicts may arise requiring formal dispute resolution, so a clearly written and agreed upon clause will serve all parties well in the long run.

### Broker's Secret >>> Counter Offers

Never reject an offer—always make a counter offer. The buyer's first offer is usually to set a baseline for the negotiation, so don't be offended, just counter back. Once a dialogue begins between you and the buyer, the goal will be to agree somewhere in the middle that feels like a win-win for both parties.

### Broker's Secret >>> Purchase Price Allocation

The Allocation of the Purchase Price for the seller must match the allocation for the buyer exactly, without exception.

### Broker's Secret >>> Business Skeletons

Due diligence is not a time for surprises. Every business has a skeleton or two, so share any problems with your broker and the buyer right away. If you reveal your concerns early in the process, you will hopefully have time to resolve the issues. However, if you wait until due diligence, that small little skeleton may suddenly become frightening enough to scare your buyer away.

### Broker's Secret >>> Corporate Minutes

Make sure your corporate minutes are current before placing your business on the market, particularly in the event of a stock sale as they will reviewed in detail during due diligence.

### Broker's Secret >>> Disclosure Statement

If your broker doesn't require you to complete a disclosure statement, get a new broker! This document, if completed honestly and updated if there are any material changes, will keep you out of court. Even if you somehow end up in a dispute, presenting your disclosure statement will probably save you thousands of dollars so NEVER skip this step!

### Broker's Secret >>> Identity Theft

Ask the buyer to black out social security numbers on his or her credit report and tax returns before providing them to you. Your broker should do the same for your tax returns. In a time when identity theft is rampant, you can never be too careful.

### Broker's Secret >>> Successor Liability

If you grow your business by acquiring assets from another company, do not buy the assets without a lien clearance. Successor liability for unknown back taxes, debts, or litigation can bankrupt you!

# Sample Valuation Worksheets

**Business A: Wholesale / Distribution Company**

**Business B: Service Company**

**Business C: Retail Store with Real Estate**

**Business D: Restaurant**

# Summary Income Statement & Seller's Discretionary Earnings

## WHOLESALE / DISTRIBUTION COMPANY

|  |  | Current Full Year | Previous Yr | Previous Yr |
|---|---|---|---|---|
| Sales |  | $4,430,503 | $4,305,018 | $3,995,180 |
| Cost of Goods Sold/Cost of Sales |  | $3,389,733 | $3,427,091 | $3,190,857 |
| Gross Profit |  | $1,040,770 | $878,226 | $804,572 |
| Other Income |  | $0 | $0 | $0 |
| Expenses |  | $928,222 | $798,578 | $658,693 |
| Net Income |  | $112,548 | $88,648 | $145,879 |
| ADJUSTMENTS |  |  |  |  |
| Depreciation |  | $38,785 | $326 | $11,749 |
| Amortization |  | $0 | $0 | $0 |
| Interest on Loans to Business from Lenders |  | $0 | $0 | $0 |
| Officer's / Owner's Salary |  | $17,160 | $17,160 | $181,896 |
| Officer's Payroll Taxes |  | $1,760 | $1,716 | $18,189 |
| Second Owner / Partner Salary |  | $190,146 | $190,146 | $22,032 |
| Second Owner / Partner Payroll Taxes |  | $19,014 | $19,014 | $2,203 |
| Auto |  | $0 | $0 | $0 |
| Insurance for Owner: Auto |  | $0 | $0 | $0 |
| Insurance for Owner: Health |  | $0 | $0 | $0 |

# WHOLESALE / DISTRIBUTION COMPANY, Continued

| | | | | |
|---|---|---|---|---|
| Insurance for Owner: Life | | $0 | $0 | $0 |
| Retirement Contributions for Owner(s) | | $177,228 | $177,228 | $102,346 |
| Second Owner Salary Adjustment | | -$55,000 | -$53,000 | -$51,000 |
| Fair Market Rent Adjustment | | $0 | $0 | $0 |
| Contributions & Donations | | $0 | $0 | $0 |
| Meals & Entertainment | | $0 | $0 | $0 |
| Travel | | $0 | $0 | $0 |
| One-Time Expenses (Renovation, Equip Purchase, Legal) | | $0 | $0 | $0 |
| **TOTAL DISCRETIONARY ADJUSTMENTMENTS** | | **$389,049** | **$352,590** | **$277,415** |
| NET INCOME | | $112,548 | $88,648 | $145,879 |
| **TOTAL SELLER'S DISCRETIONARY EARNINGS** | | **$501,597** | **$441,238** | **$423,294** |
| *Inventory Included* | *$300,000* | | | |
| *Equipment Included* | *$50,000* | | | |
| *Receivables Included* | *$300,000* | | | |
| **MARKET OPINION OF VALUE** | **$2,420,000 - $2,650,000** | | | |

# Summary Income Statement & Seller's Discretionary Earnings

## SERVICE COMPANY

| | | Current Full Year | Previous Yr | Previous Yr |
|---|---|---|---|---|
| Sales | | $2,802,358 | $2,495,721 | $2,908,531 |
| Cost of Goods Sold/Cost of Sales | | $1,123,196 | $1,461,287 | $1,197,926 |
| Gross Profit | | $1,679,161 | $1,796,863 | $1,710,605 |
| Other Income | | $0 | $0 | $0 |
| Expenses | | $1,556,181 | $1,697,923 | $1,613,906 |
| Net Income | | $124,006 | $88,806 | $96,738 |
| ADJUSTMENTS | | | | |
| Depreciation | | $1,783 | $39,591 | $0 |
| Armortization | | $1,045 | $1,609 | $995 |
| Interest on Loans to Business from Lenders | | $150,000 | $163,750 | $148,750 |
| Officer's / Owner's Salary | | $15,000 | $16,375 | $14,875 |
| Officer's Paroll Taxes | | $0 | $0 | $0 |
| Second Owner/ Partner Salary | | $0 | $0 | $0 |
| Second Owner/ Parnter Payroll Taxes | | $0 | $0 | $0 |
| Auto | | $0 | $0 | $0 |
| Insurance for Owner: Auto | | $0 | $0 | $0 |
| Insurance for Owner: Health | | $0 | $0 | $0 |

## SERVICE COMPANY, Continued

| | | | | |
|---|---|---|---|---|
| Insurance for Owner: Life | | $0 | $0 | $0 |
| Retirement Contributions for Owner(s) | | $0 | $0 | $0 |
| Second Owner Salary Adjustment | | $0 | $0 | $0 |
| Fair Market Rent Adjustment | | $85,641 | $76,486 | $149,863 |
| Contributions & Donations | | $2,896 | $4,958 | $2,640 |
| Meals & Entertainment | | | | |
| Travel | | | | |
| One-Time Expenses (Renovation, Equip Purchase, Legal) | | $2,000 | $0 | $10,882 |
| **TOTAL DISCRETIONARY ADJUSTMENTS** | | **$258,365** | **$302,769** | **$327,965** |
| NET INCOME | | $124,006 | $88,806 | $96,738 |
| **TOTAL SELLERS DISCRETIONARY EARNINGS** | | **$382,371** | **$391,575** | **$424,703** |
| *Inventory Included* | *$1,100* | | | |
| *Equipment Included* | *$174,452* | | | |
| **MARKET OPINION OF VALUE** | **$1,200,000** | | | |

# Summary Income Statement & Seller's Discretionary Earnings

## RETAIL STORE with Real Estate (Building)

| | | Current Full Year | Previous Yr | Previous Yr |
|---|---|---|---|---|
| Sales | | $333,935 | $486,508 | $345,054 |
| Cost of Goods Sold/Cost of Sales | | $169,835 | $302,641 | $216,202 |
| Gross Profit | | $163,685 | $183,867 | $128,852 |
| Other Income | | $0 | $0 | $0 |
| Expenses | | $102,181 | $111,601 | $96,013 |
| Net Income | | $61,502 | $72,266 | $32,839 |
| ADJUSTMENTS | | | | |
| Depreciation | | $12,764 | $22,273 | $10,370 |
| Amortization | | | | |
| Interest on Loans to Business from Lenders | | $24,082 | $30,710 | $30,963 |
| Officer's / Owner's Salary | | $0 | $0 | $0 |
| Officer's Payroll Taxes | | $0 | $0 | $0 |
| Second Owner / Partner Salary | | $0 | $0 | $0 |
| Second Owner / Partner Payroll Taxes | | $0 | $0 | $0 |
| Auto | | $0 | $0 | $0 |
| Insurance for Owner: Auto | | $0 | $0 | $0 |
| Insurance for Owner: Health | | $3,800 | $3,800 | $0 |
| Insurance for Owner: Life | | $0 | $0 | $0 |

## RETAIL STORE with Real Estate (Building), Continued

| | | | | |
|---|---|---|---|---|
| Retirement Contributions for Owner(s) | | $0 | $0 | $0 |
| Second Owner Salary Adjustment | | $0 | $0 | $0 |
| Fair Market Rent Adjustment | | $0 | $0 | $0 |
| Contributions & Donations | | $0 | $0 | $0 |
| Meals & Entertainment | | $0 | $0 | $0 |
| Travel | | $0 | $0 | $0 |
| One-Time Expenses (Renovation, Equip Purchase, Legal) | | $0 | $0 | $0 |
| **TOTAL DISCRETIONARY ADJUSTMENTMENTS** | | **$40,556** | **$56,783** | **$41,333** |
| NET INCOME | | $61,502 | $72,266 | $32,839 |
| **TOTAL SELLER'S DISCRETIONARY EARNINGS** | | **$102,058** | **$129,049** | **$74,172** |
| *Inventory Included* | *$100,000* | | | |
| *Equipment Included* | *$10,000* | | | |
| *Real Estate Included* | *$800,000* | | | |
| **MARKET OPINION OF VALUE** | **$1,100,000** | | | |
| *($300,000 Business, $800,000 Building)* | | | | |

# Summary Income Statement & Seller's Discretionary Earnings

## RESTAURANT

|  |  | Current Full Year | Previous Yr | *Start-up* Previous Yr* |
|---|---|---|---|---|
| Sales |  | $455,757 | $368,285 | $150,045 |
| Cost of Goods Sold/Cost of Sales |  | $169,956 | $143,390 | $45,057 |
| Gross Profit |  | $254,063 | $224,099 | $104,988 |
| Other Income |  | $0 | $0 | $0 |
| Expenses |  | $277,802 | $249,461 | $131,806 |
| Net Income |  | ($23,739) | ($25,362) | ($26,818) |
| ADJUSTMENTS |  |  |  |  |
| Depreciation |  | $20,433 | $8,188 | $0 |
| Amortization |  |  | $1,187 | $0 |
| Interest on Loans to Business from Lenders |  | $11,661 | $23,469 | $4,065 |
| Officer's / Owner's Salary |  | $36,000 | $36,000 | $36,000 |
| Officer's Payroll Taxes |  | $0 | $0 | $0 |
| Second Owner / Partner Salary |  | $0 | $0 | $0 |
| Second Owner / Partner Payroll Taxes |  | $0 | $0 | $0 |
| Auto |  | $0 | $0 | $0 |
| Insurance for Owner: Auto |  | $8,340 | $8,340 | $8,340 |

## RESTAURANT, Continued

| | | | | |
|---|---|---|---|---|
| Insurance for Owner: Health | | $5,112 | $5,112 | $5,112 |
| Insurance for Owner: Life | | $900 | $900 | $900 |
| Retirement Contributions for Owner(s) | | $0 | $0 | $0 |
| Second Owner Salary Adjustment | | $0 | $0 | $0 |
| Fair Market Rent Adjustment | | $0 | $0 | $0 |
| Contributions & Donations | | $0 | $248 | $115 |
| Meals & Entertainment | | $4,446 | $2,128 | $1,320 |
| Travel | | $0 | $0 | $0 |
| One-Time Expenses (Renovation, Equip Purchase, Legal) | | $0 | $0 | $0 |
| **TOTAL DISCRETIONARY ADJUSTMENTMENTS** | | **$86,892** | **$85,572** | **$55,852** |
| NET INCOME | | ($23,739) | ($25,362) | ($26,818) |
| **TOTAL SELLER'S DISCRETIONARY EARNINGS** | | **$63,153** | **$60,210** | **$29,034** |
| *Inventory Included* | *$3,500* | | | |
| *Equipment Included* | *$16,000* | | | |
| **MARKET OPINION OF VALUE** | **$145,000** | | | |

# Valuation Worksheet

Business owners should understand the value of their business at all times.

What if you receive an unsolicited offer from a competitor?

What if you experience a partnership dispute, divorce, or tragic death and need to know the value of your business now?

I don't want you to ever have to worry or be forced to pay possibly thousands of dollars for a valuation when if you only had the tools, you could calculate a fairly accurate market opinion of value in thirty minutes or less.

To receive your complimentary Valuation Worksheet with built-in formulas, go to www.exitjourney.com/worksheet and a link to the downloadable file will be emailed to you right away.

Enjoy!

# 11 Deal Breakers to Dodge

1. Don't become emotional and overprice your business.

2. Don't forget to meet with your accountant to understand the tax consequences of the sale of your business.

3. Don't go to market without a complete marketing package, including three years of financial statements ready for potential buyers to review.

4. Don't share confidential information about your business with buyers unless they have signed a confidentiality agreement and are financially and professionally qualified.

5. Don't let your sales drop after you put your business on the market.

6. Don't leave deferred maintenance for a buyer because curb appeal counts in business sales, too.

7. Don't rely on your competitors to be your only potential buyers.

8. Don't wait for an offer to determine if the lease for your space is transferable.

9. Don't give a buyer access to all of your financial, customer, and/or employee records until you have agreed in writing on the price and terms of the sale.

10. Don't accept an offer without a substantial good faith deposit.

11. Never tell your employees or customers that the business is being sold, because it's never over until you have the check in hand!

# How to Select a Qualified Business Broker

1. Ask for references from previous sellers and buyers.

2. Ask if the broker will value the business before it goes to market.

3. Ask which professional organizations the broker belongs to and if he or she has earned any certifications from those organizations.

4. Ask if the broker will "cooperate or co-broker" (work with and share fees) with another broker who may have a buyer.

5. Ask if the broker will represent you exclusively or both parties as a dual agent.

6. Ask what the fee is for a transaction your size.

7. Ask how the broker will market the business for sale.

8. Determine how frequently the broker will communicate with you regarding the status of your transaction.

9. Ask to review the Representation Agreement in advance of the day of signing.

10. After doing your homework, your final decision is to determine if the broker you are considering is someone you can trust and work with closely for the next six to twelve months.

# Recommended Reading List

*One Page Business Plan by Jim Horan*
A classic and the perfect platform from which to launch, reflect, or strategize.

*Mastering the Rockefeller Habits by Verne Harnish*
An excellent blueprint to grow your small business into the stratosphere in manageable quarterly increments.

*Built to Sell by John Warillow*
This book is part one, and my book is the sequel. John has grown and sold several of his own businesses and does an excellent job of showing how to add value to your company from an owner's perspective.

*E-Myth Mastery by Michael Gerber*
Another classic not to be missed.

*The Ultimate Sales Machine by Chet Holmes*
Chet is a sales genius and clearly lays out a plan to hire superstars and double your sales. The hard part is sticking to the plan!

*Crush It! by Gary Vaynerchuk*
If you love social media like I love social media, you have to read Gary's book!

*MothersWork by Rebecca Matthias*
One of my very favorite business books detailing Rebecca Matthias's struggle to take a home-based maternity business all the way to a public company with three babies in tow. I think I have read this book at least three times!

*The One Minute Millionaire by Robert G. Allen and Mark Victor Hansen*
If you had to make a million dollars in ninety days to save your family, what would you do? This book inspired me to get focused and stop wasting time!

# Coaching, Seminars, Speaking, and Social Media

## EXIT! Seminar Series

After reading the book, you may need a hands-on intensive review, so I am offering ongoing online coaching and multi-day seminars so you can go to the next level of understanding and really apply what you have learned. For more information, go to www.exitjourney.com.

## Speaking

I frequently speak about selling businesses, buying businesses, growing businesses, growing families, and social media. I am available for keynotes and workshops, and my audiences have ranged from the Women Presidents' Organization to Mergers & Acquisitions Source. For more information, email to speak@exitjourncy.com to receive a speaker's package with booking information and rates.

## Blog and Website

www.exitjourney.com

## LinkedIn

www.linkedin.com/in/juliegordonwhite

## Facebook

www.facebook.com/juliegordonwhite

## Twitter

www.twitter.com/pinkbizbroker

# Fundraising with This Book

I am on a mission to teach 10,000,000 entrepreneurs how to sell their businesses for the price they deserve. In order to do so, I would love to gift your organization with a wholesale price to not only share the message, but also help generate revenue for your organization. The minimum order is 100 books. Email fundraising@theexitbook.com for details or complete and fax back the order form below.

## My organization would like to fundraise with EXIT!

We are ordering (check one):
- ☐ 100 books
- ☐ 200 books
- ☐ 500 books
- ☐ Other_____

Please contact me to confirm my order of _____ books times $____ for a total of $_____. My contact info is:

Name_____
Organization _____
Address _____
City _____ State _____ Zip Code _____
Phone Number _____
Email Address _____

**FAX this order request attention: Bulk EXIT! Purchase 510.217.4464**

Made in the USA
Lexington, KY
08 February 2012